Proof of Moral Obligation in Twentieth-Century Philosophy

American University Studies

Series V
Philosophy

Vol. 45

PETER LANG
New York · Bern · Frankfurt am Main · Paris

Paul Allen III

Proof of Moral Obligation
in Twentieth-Century Philosophy

PETER LANG
New York · Bern · Frankfurt am Main · Paris

Library of Congress Cataloging-in-Publication Data

Allen, Paul.
Proof of moral obligation in twentieth-century philosophy.

(American university studies. Series V, Philosophy ; vol. 45)
1. Ethics, Modern—20th century. I. Title.
II. Series: American university studies. Series V, Philosophy ; v. 45.
BJ319.A43   1988   170'.9'04   87-29333
ISBN 0-8204-0568-X
ISSN 0739-6406

CIP-Titelaufnahme der Deutschen Bibliothek

Allen, Paul:
Proof of moral obligation in twentieth-century philosophy / Paul Allen. – New York; Bern; Frankfurt am Main; Paris: Lang, 1988.
 (American University Studies: Ser, 5, Philosophy; Vol. 45)
 ISBN 0-8204-0568-X

NE: American University Studies / 05

© Peter Lang Publishing, Inc., New York 1988

All rights reserved.
Reprint or reproduction, even partially, in all forms such as microfilm, xerography, microfiche, microcard, offset strictly prohibited.

Printed by Weihert-Druck GmbH, Darmstadt, West Germany

To
James R. Kuehl
and the late Robert E. McClary

Contents

Preface xi

PART ONE
MAJOR ACCOUNTS OF JUSTIFICATION IN ETHICS,
1900–1960

I History of Justification: Moore's Critique of the
   Naturalists....................................... 3
   The Purpose of This Study 3
   Justification in Naturalistic and Metaphysical
      Theories of Ethics............................ 5
   Mill... 5
   Aristotle 7
   Conclusions About Naturalistic and Metaphysical
      Theories 9
   Moore's Criticism of Naturalistic and Metaphysical
      Theories 12
   How Moore Accounts for Ultimate Justification 14

II History of Justification (Continued): Prichard, Ayer,
   Stevenson, and the Analysts...................... 17
   Prichard's Critique of Moore 17
   How Prichard Accounts for Ultimate Justification .. 20
   Ayer's Criticism of Prichard..................... 21
   Does Ayer's Emotivism Help Account for
      Justification? 27
   A Note on Stevenson............................. 27
   The Rise of Analysis 30

III Toulmin: Social Harmony as the Basis of Justification .. 37
    Toulmin's Attack on the Earlier Theories 37

	Toulmin's Fresh Approach to the Problem of	
	Justification	40
	Reasons in Science...........................	41
	Reasons in Ethics	44
	Ultimate Justification	48
IV	**Toulmin (Continued): Challenges From Hare**.........	**55**
	The Nature of Communal Life as an Objective Basis for Justification......................	55
	Hare's Argument That Toulmin Cannot Derive Obligation From Facts......................	59
	Criteria to Clarify the Idea of Ultimate Justification	65
	A Dilemma: Arbitrary Premises or Non-Moral Ones	67

PART TWO
HARE'S ANALYSIS OF MORAL JUSTIFICATION

V	**Hare's *The Language of Morals*: How We Deduce Moral Principles.............................**	**75**
	There Can Be Valid Deduction From Prescriptive Premises	75
	Prescriptive and Factual Premises Are Both Needed	79
	Unlike Descriptivism, Prescriptivism Allows for Moral *Decision*	83
	Decisions of Principle May Be Justified, Thanks to Deduction and Facts	87
VI	**Hare's *The Language of Morals* (Continued): Are Our Moral Decisions Fully Justified?**	**91**
	Does Attention to Facts Keep Principles From Being Arbitrary?..............................	91
	Has Hare Explained Away the Factor of Decision?.	94
	Are Decisions Justified Thanks to Logic, Principles, and Facts?	96
	Dependence on Prior Principles Would Keep a Principle Partly Uncertain.....................	99

Contents

VII	**Hare's *Freedom and Reason:* Justification as a Function of Logical Consistency**	105
	Moral Reasoning Is Testing Principles by Checking Consequences	105
	To Check Consequences, We Must Consider Being in the Other's Shoes	110
	Must One Face the Unpleasant Logical Consequences?	113
	The Certainty of Moral Justification Is Logical, Not Just Factual	116
VIII	**Hare's *Freedom and Reason* (Continued): The Role of Inclinations in Justification**	119
	The Factors Relevant to Formulating a Principle Are Those Used in the Original Judgment	119
	Our Inclinations Determine What Consequences We Will Put Up With	123
	Hare's Emphasis on Inclinations Helps Him Explain Practical Application	126
	Inclination and Exploration Help to Account for Individual Choice	127
	Variations in Inclinations Need Not Lead to Disorder in Society	131
	Fanatics Escape Censure. Is This a Flaw in Hare's Theory?	134
	A Note About Hare's Other Books	137

PART THREE
COMPLETING THE ACCOUNT OF ULTIMATE JUSTIFICATION

IX	**Building on Hare With Help From Gewirth**	143
	One Thing No One Will Ever Give Up Is "Immediate Freedom"	144
	Logic Requires Us to Prescribe Others' Freedom As Well As Our Own	146
	We Will Give Up Future Prerogatives but Not Immediate Freedom	147

	We *Cannot* Give Up Immediate Freedom: Deciding to Act Presupposes It................................	151
	Have We Derived an "Ought" From an "Is"?.....	153
X	**Practical Application and Summary**..................	**159**
	Our Theory Labels Nothing Good or Bad, but Still Gives Guidance...............................	159
	Although Hard Cases Spark Debate, We *Have* Accounted for Ultimate Justification	162
	Recapitulation	166
Index	....	173

PREFACE

Although this book is intended primarily for philosophers and graduate students, several readers have described the style of writing as especially clear and easy to follow. This prompts me to caution philosophers who are glancing through it: Please do not let the deceptively simple style of writing mislead you into assuming that this is primarily a student text. Although Chapters 1 and 2 are a historical survey, I trust that from Chapter 3 on, you will find plenty of fresh and challenging philosophical analysis.

At the same time, the easy style does qualify the book as a text for upper level ethics courses.

One suggestion for professors who adopt it for their courses: If you find it necessary to assign your class less than the full book, Chapters 5 and 6 (on Hare's *The Language of Morals*) may be the ones to skip. The reader can proceed from Chapter 4 to Chapter 7 and still follow most of the important threads of the overall argument.

I would like to acknowledge and give thanks to: my colleagues Gordon Brumm, David Forth, George Thompson, and James Hall for their help and support; Kathryn Murray for a great deal of valuable work on the index, proofreading, and many other large and small projects; Judith DeCamp for her editorial expertise and cooperative spirit; Jay Wilson for understanding and encouragement; Paul Hofmann for his guidance; Ian MacLachlan *et al* for great care and skill; Theresa Gress for the good typing job; my wife Gretchen for much valuable editorial assistance and other kinds of support and advice; and my daughter Daphne and son Brent for their help and patience.

P.A.

Part One

Major Accounts of Justification in Ethics, 1900–1960

I

History of Justification: Moore's Critique of the Naturalists

THE PURPOSE OF THIS STUDY

All of us from time to time believe that we are morally bound to do a particular act. That is, we believe we are obligated in an overriding or absolute way to keep a promise, join the army, evade the draft, give up drinking, or whatever it may be. In such instances, it should be possible to explain our obligation by giving reasons or an explanation which is satisfactory and complete. If the reasons given for doing the act are in some way inadequate or incomplete, then it seems that our obligation to do the act will be less than fully demonstrated.

Throughout this book when referring to an explanation or set of reasons for doing an act, we will use the term "justification." And to refer to a justification which could be described as adequate, complete, and absolute, we will use the term "ultimate justification." To be ultimate, then, a justification must not depend on additional justification; that is, it must not consist of reasons which are dependent on further reasons. For if it did, the agent could still have a least some doubt as to whether he was morally required in an overriding way to do the act in question. Thus, for a justification to be ultimate, there must be no room for any doubt or further questioning about whether the agent is absolutely morally bound to do that act. In short, an ultimate justification can be thought of as a thorough demonstration or *proof* that one is morally required to do the act under consideration.

Throughout the centuries when working on ethics, philosophers have largely ignored the problem of proving that we are subject to moral obligation. Instead, they have concentrated mostly on the question of *which* acts are morally obligatory. However, in this study, we will pay very little attention to which acts or what kinds of behavior are obligatory. Thus, our focus will be on the nature of the ultimate justification itself, not on what sort of acts it justifies.

Our method of searching for an account of ultimate justification will be to analyze various philosophers' theories which come close to being such a proof—our hope being that this process will eventually lead to a full-fledged proof of moral obligation.

But as we analyze one theory of justification after another, we will be accomplishing something else as well: We will be developing a clearer idea of what an ultimate justification—or proof of moral obligation—would be like.

The philosopher whose theory of justification will be analyzed most deeply is R. M. Hare. And because our scope must be limited, most of our other philosophers will also be twentieth-century thinkers—people whose contributions on the subject of ultimate justification are especially significant: Moore, Prichard, Ayer, Stevenson, Toulmin, and Gewirth.

A further reason for selecting these particular philosophers is not only that each of them presents a clearcut explanation of justification (except Ayer and Stevenson), but also that most of them give an explicit refutation of the previous person's account. Accordingly, we will begin each philosopher with an investigation of his critique of the one before him, and then turn to his own attempt to explain ultimate justification. For example, when we get to Prichard, we will first examine how he attacks Moore's account of justification and then how he replaces it with his own.

Thus, through these philosophers, we will be tracing the evolution of some prevailing views on ultimate justification in England and America since the beginning of this century. Although tracing this historical theme provides a valuable framework on which the reader can build further historical knowledge, our purpose is not to construct a complete or balanced history of twentieth-century ethics. Again, our main purpose will be to find an account of ultimate justification, i.e., a proof of moral obligation.

JUSTIFICATION IN NATURALISTIC AND METAPHYSICAL THEORIES OF ETHICS

Before starting our first twentieth-century thinker, G. E. Moore (1873–1958), it is necessary to characterize the kind of ethical systems which elicited his analysis. I will select two philosophers who I feel are the most representative of the leading traditional schools of the type Moore was criticizing, and whose accounts of ultimate justification are especially clearcut—namely, Mill and Aristotle.

Mill

If we asked John Stuart Mill (1806–1873) to justify a certain act of his, he would say he did the act because he expected it to produce pleasure. He would also add various qualifications regarding the number of individuals the pleasure would reach and the quality of the pleasure; but for our present purposes, we can ignore such considerations.

If we then asked Mill what justification or reasons he had for promoting pleasure, he might reply as follows:

> The utilitarian doctrine is that happiness is desirable, and the only thing desirable, as an end; all other things being only desirable as means to that end. What ought to be required of this doctrine, what conditions is it requisite that the doctrine should fulfill—to make good its claim to be believed?
>
> The only proof capable of being given that an object is visible is that people actually see it. . . .the sole evidence it is possible to produce that anything is desirable is that people do actually desire it. . . .No reason can be given why the general happiness is desirable, except that each person, so far as he believes it to be attainable, desires his own happiness. This, however, being a fact, we have not only all the proof which the case admits of, but all which it is possible to require, that happiness is a good.[1]

Regardless of what flaws we may find in Mill's reasoning, he seems to be making a definite claim to base his system on a kind of justification which is ultimate or final in the sense that there is no need to seek further reasons.

He admits a few sentences earlier, "that questions of ultimate ends do not admit of proof, in the ordinary acceptation of the term. To be incapable of proof by reasoning is common to all first principles."[2] But regardless of whether his argument can be called a proof in the usual sense, it is clear that Mill believes that he has given us a justification for hedonism which does not depend on further evidence or reasons. In fact, later on he reiterates: "If human nature is so constituted as to desire nothing which is not either a part of happiness or a means of happiness—we can have no other proof, and we require no other, that these are the only things desirable. If so, happiness is the sole end of human action."[3]

Thus, Mill and the other hedonists who subscribe to his reasoning on this point believe that their theory avoids an infinite regress of hypothetical imperatives: If it can be established that an act produces more pleasure than pain (and perhaps that it meets certain other criteria regarding the number of people affected and the quality of the pleasure, etc.), then the act would seem fully justified. That is to say, one does not have to give further reasons why pleasure is the proper goal of human action. Since one's seeking of reasons or justification can stop at this point, one has produced the sort of justification which we are calling ultimate—or so Mill would have us believe.

Aristotle

For Aristotle (384–322 B.C.), on the other hand, the proper goal for human beings is not happiness in the sense of pleasure as Mill claimed; rather it is happiness in the sense of well-being or fulfillment (eudaimonia). Pleasure is merely a by-product. But how do we find out what constitutes well-being? Quoting Aristotle:

> To say however that the Supreme Good is happiness will probably appear a truism; we still require a more explicit account of what constitutes happiness. Perhaps then we may arrive at this by ascertaining what is man's function. For the goodness or efficiency of a flute-player or sculptor or craftsman of any sort, and in general of anybody who has some function or business to perform, is thought to reside in that function;

and similarly it may be held that the good of man resides in the function of man, if he has a function.[4]

Aristotle proceeds to figure out what our function is by analyzing human nature. He finds out that the function special to human beings, as contrasted with lower forms of life, is rationality. To fulfill this function of rationality, we must live a life of high quality intellectual activity—what Aristotle calls "intellectual virtue."

But human beings also share some lower level functions with plant life and with the non-rational animals—such as nutrition, growth and reproduction, and perception, appetite and mobility. Fulfillment or proper handling of appetites and other bodily functions requires that we control and moderate them by means of good habits, and according to rational principles. Such moderating of appetites and other bodily functions is called "moral virtue" by Aristotle.

According to Aristotle, then, to achieve happiness in the sense of fulfillment, we have to live a life of intellectual and moral virtue. Aristotle believes that this happiness is the *ultimate* good in the sense that it does not require further justification. In his words,

> ... a thing chosen always as an end and never as a means we call absolutely final. Now happiness above all else appears to be absolutely final in this sense, since we always choose it for its own sake and never as a means to something else.[5]
>
> Happiness, therefore, being found to be something final and self-sufficient, is the End at which all actions aim.[6]

Thus we can interpret Aristotle as meaning that if it could be established that a certain act or way of living would maximize human happiness, or well-being, the act would be fully justified. That is, the principle "seek well-being" does not itself require further justification. Alasdair MacIntyre puts it this way:

> Clearly, Aristotle is saying that the *concept* of happiness is such that we could not use it of anything but a final end. Equally, happiness is a self-sufficient good . . . . Thus, to justify some action by saying "Happiness is brought by this" or "Happiness consists in doing this" is always to give a reason for acting which terminates argument. No further *why?* can be raised.[7]

Accordingly, Aristotle, like Mill, believes that he has founded his ethics on a principle which is ultimate in the sense that it needs no further reasons or justification to support it.

CONCLUSIONS ABOUT NATURALISTIC AND METAPHYSICAL THEORIES

We can classify Aristotle's and Mill's theories as "naturalistic" if we follow G. E. Moore's definition:

> Those theories of Ethics, then, are 'naturalistic' which declare the sole good to consist in some one property of things, which exists in time; and which do so because they suppose that 'good' itself can be defined by reference to such a property.[8]

And of course, many other traditional theories fall into Moore's naturalistic category, e.g., the various schools of hedonism other than Mill's, interest theories like that of R. B. Perry, and evolutionary theories such as Spencer's.

Although there is not room to discuss more of these naturalistic theories individually here, it seems safe to say that most if not all of them share with Aristotle and Mill the feature we have been pointing out. That is to say, naturalistic theories take some property or thing within nature (e.g., pleasure, well-being, satisfying of interest,[9] or conforming to evolutionary trends), and consider it to be the authentic and fully adequate basis for moral justification. In other words, after showing us the significance of pleasure, fulfillment, or whatever, and after explaining that its importance or value obligates us to do acts which promote it, the philosopher believes that he has accounted for moral justification in a way that can be called ultimate.

Something similar can be said about the ethical systems which Moore calls metaphysical. He defines "metaphysical systems" this way:

> . . . those systems of Ethics, which I propose to call 'Metaphysical,' are characterised by the fact that they describe the Supreme Good. . . in terms of something which (they hold) does exist, but does not exist in Nature—in terms of a supersensible reality.[10]

And he proceeds to cite examples of metaphysical theories of ethics:

> Such an assertion was made by the Stoics when they asserted that a life in accordance with Nature was perfect. For they did not mean by 'Nature,' what I have so defined, but something supersensible which they inferred to exist, and which they held to be perfectly good. Such an assertion, again, is made by Spinoza when he tells us that we are more or less perfect, in proportion as we are more or less closely united with Absolute Substance by the 'intellectual love' of God. Such an assertion

is made by Kant when he tells us that his 'Kingdom of Ends' is the ideal. And such, finally, is made by modern writers who tell us that the final and perfect end is to realize our *true* selves—a self different both from the whole and from any part of that which exists here and now in Nature.[11]

It is beyond the scope of this chapter to discuss in detail the theories cited by Moore, or other theories which would fall into his "metaphysical" category, such as various versions of Platonic, Christian, and Thomistic theories. Nevertheless, I believe the reader will agree that Spinoza, Stoics, Thomists, and other metaphysical moralists, no less than naturalists like Mill, consider their supreme good (be it Nature, Absolute Substance, or realization of one's *true* self) to be ultimate in the sense that it does not derive its value from something still higher. For example, consider the "modern writers" Moore referred to above "who tell us that the final and perfect end is to realize our *true* selves." No doubt these philosophers would say that a certain person's way of life was *fully* justified if it realized that person's *true* self (and if it met certain other requirements, such as not conflicting with the realization of others' true selves).

To summarize these comments about naturalistic and metaphysical theories, as a rule when a philosopher establishes that a certain property, state, or thing is the supreme good (be it inside or outside of nature), he is conceiving of its value as self-sufficient, i.e., as not dependent on some still higher good or principle. Thus, when a decision, act, or way of life is justified in terms of that supreme good, it has ultimate justification according to that theory.

MOORE'S CRITICISM OF NATURALISTIC AND METAPHYSICAL THEORIES

Until the present century, most ethical theories have been either naturalistic or metaphysical. However, all of these attempts to account for ultimate justification fail according to G. E. Moore's analysis—and always for the same reason, viz., that they commit the "naturalistic fallacy." Since Moore's naturalistic fallacy argument is well known, a brief sketch of it here will do:

Early in the first chapter of *Principia Ethica*, Moore asserts that the most fundamental question in ethics is not which thing or things are good, but how "good" is to be defined.[12] He then claims that, contrary to what most philosophers have thought, "good" is not definable at all. He argues that it is useless for ethics to try to define "good" by merely offering synonyms for the word "good." That method of defining does not get at the meaning of the word; it merely substitutes one symbol for another. It evades the issue because it does not identify the property which "good" designates. An adequate definition would have to be a *description* of the properties or other elements referred to by the word.[13]

But to give such a descriptive definition of "good" is impossible because this word does not even refer to a set of properties or elements; it denotes a simple quality. We can give descriptive definitions of words standing for complex objects such as a horse because such things can be described by enumerating their elements. But "good" and certain other words, such as "yellow," refer to simple qualities which cannot be broken down into parts and thus cannot be described or defined.[14]

Of course, we can *correlate* the simple quality yellow with a specific kind of light vibration which is a complex thing. But because yellow is a simple quality, we cannot *identify* it with those light waves. Similarly, it is fallacious to say that goodness *is* pleasure or any other thing inside or outside of nature except goodness itself. Pleasure may be good in the sense of having goodness, but it cannot be *identified* with goodness. If the two were identical, saying "pleasure is good" would amount to saying "pleasure is pleasure."[15]

This leads us to Moore's so-called "open question argument." Suppose that the hedonist claims that "good" means "pleasure." We may agree that a certain act is pleasant, yet ask, "This is pleasant, but is it good?" However, if "good" meant "pleasant," our question would be equivalent to "This is pleasant, but is it pleasant?" and we would be talking nonsense, which obviously we are not. Thus, the fact that we can intelligibly ask of pleasure, well-being, realization of one's true self, etc., "Is it good?" shows that "good" *means* none of these things.[16]

Therefore, to identify good with anything such as pleasure or self-realization is a fallacy according to Moore.[17] The most we can say is that things like pleasure can be good in the sense that they *have* goodness but not in the sense that they *are* goodness. The goodness which they have is a quality which is itself simple and indefinable.

In pointing out that a property such as pleasure is not identified with but merely *has* goodness, Moore is showing that pleasure (or whatever) is not the ultimate basis of moral justification. The value of pleasure depends on something else, viz., the indefinable quality goodness. Therefore, even if the hedonist is right in saying that we ought to be kind because kind acts promote pleasure, in saying this, he has not given a *full* explanation of why we should be kind. For his justification to be complete, he must add that pleasure is to be promoted because it possesses goodness.

Similarly with any of the other naturalistic or metaphysical theories we have mentioned. If well-being or realization of one's true self is a proper end for action, this can be established only by appeal to something else: the indefinable quality good which it possesses. Since naturalistic and metaphysical theories have not taken this further step of appealing to the indefinable good, none of them accounts for ultimate justification.

HOW MOORE ACCOUNTS FOR ULTIMATE JUSTIFICATION

Of course, Moore's analysis of ethics is not purely negative. On the positive side, he has offered a new theory which provides a fresh explanation of ultimate justification. His theory essentially is that good is a real quality which is simple and indefinable but which we can *intuit*. We can intuit that certain things such as the pleasures of human intercourse and the enjoyment of beautiful objects are good—in that they *have* goodness, not that they are identical to it.[18] It then follows that acts which tend to promote good things are right, i.e., they ought to be done.

For Moore, the value or moral significance of that indefinable quality, goodness, on which the goodness or rightness of acts depends, does not depend in turn on anything higher than itself. Therefore, when an act can be shown to maximize goodness, it would seem that the agent is morally bound to do the act—i.e., that that particular act for that agent has ultimate justification. Accordingly, Moore seems to have succeeded in giving us an account of ultimate justification.

* * *

Incidentally, the foregoing discussion has shed light on the concept of ultimate justification. It has become clear that for a justification of moral obligation to be ultimate, one criterion it must meet is this: It must not depend on an identification of goodness with pleasure, fulfillment, God's will, or any other natural or metaphysical quality or thing. In short, it must not commit the naturalistic fallacy.

NOTES

[1] J. S. Mill, *Utilitarianism* (Indianapolis: Bobbs-Merrill, 1957), p. 44.

[2] *Ibid.*, p. 44.

[3] *Ibid.*, p. 48.

[4] Aristotle, *Nicomachean Ethics* i. 7. 1097b., trans. H. Rackham (Loeb Classics; Cambridge, Mass.: Harvard University Press, 1956), p. 31.

[5] *Ibid.*, i. 7. 1097a. (Rackham, p. 27).

[6] *Ibid.*, i. 7. 1097b. (Rackham, p. 31).

[7] Alasdair MacIntyre, *A Short History of Ethics* (New York: Macmillan, 1966), p. 62.

[8] G. E. Moore, *Principia Ethica* (Cambridge: Cambridge Univ. Press, 1966), p. 41.

[9] Cf. Ralph Barton Perry, *General Theory of Value* (Cambridge, Mass.: Harvard University Press, 1926), p. 115: "This, then, we take to be the original source and constant feature of all value. That which is an object of interest is *eo ipso* invested with value. Any object, whatever it be, acquires value when any interest, whatever it be, is taken in it; just as anything whatsoever becomes a target when anyone whatsoever aims at it." See also p. 116: "In short,

interest being constitutive of value in the basic sense, theory of value will take this as its point of departure and centre of reference; and will classify and systematize values in terms of the different forms which interests and their objects may be found to assume." Cf. also: "Duty is derived from the good, and the good is relative to interests." Perry, *Realms of Value* (Cambridge: Harvard, 1954), p. 112.

[10] Moore, p. 113.

[11] *Ibid.*

[12] Moore, pp. 4–5.

[13] *Ibid.*, pp. 6 and 8.

[14] *Ibid.*, p. 7.

[15] *Ibid.*, p. 10.

[16] *Ibid.*, p. 15.

[17] For a summary of criticisms of Moore's discussion of the naturalistic fallacy, see W. K. Frankena, *Ethics* (Englewood Cliffs, N. J.: Prentice-Hall, Inc., 1963), pp. 82–83.

[18] Moore, p. 188.

II

History of Justification (Continued): Prichard, Ayer, Stevenson, and The Analysts

PRICHARD'S CRITIQUE OF MOORE

Moore proceeded from his "discovery" of the indefinable quality good to the conclusion that we ought to promote this good. Thus, if the pleasures of human interaction are good, then Moore infers that one *ought* to promote them. But such an inference is unwarranted, says H. A. Prichard (1871–1947). In Prichard's words, such a view

> contends that if something which is not an action is good, then we *ought* to undertake the action which will, directly or indirectly, originate it.
>
> But this argument, if it is to restore the sense of obligation to act, must presuppose an intermediate link, viz. the further thesis that what is good ought to be. The necessity of this link is obvious.[1]

Thus, although Moore's theory may succeed in accounting for an ultimate *end* for action (namely, the indefinable good) it leaves another gap: it does not explain why one ought to do those acts which bring about the good. I may believe that the pleasures of human interaction are good, but I may still question whether I am obligated to act to promote them. Accordingly, it seems that if Moore's theory is to give a full justification as to why we ought to act a certain way, it must close this gap, i.e., it must explain why good implies ought.

But nowhere in *Principia Ethica* does Moore account for such a link. Indeed, he thinks one is unnecessary. In one passage,[2] Moore implies that a link is unnecessary because there is no gap between good and ought; and that there is no gap because the two ideas are essentially equivalent, or at least "ought" is defined in terms of "good." Prichard quotes from this passage in Moore's book and explains how Moore is wrong to define "ought" in terms of "good."

> Professor Moore says: . . . 'What I wish first to point out is that "right" does and can mean nothing but "cause of a good result", and is thus identical with "useful".' . . . And a little later he says: 'Our "duty", therefore, can only be defined as that action, which will cause more good to exist in the Universe than any possible alternative.'
>
> Here the context shows that Professor Moore is using 'right' as the equivalent of 'ought' or 'duty'. Hence, in the sentence just quoted he is in effect asserting that the statement, 'I ought to do an act of a certain kind', e.g. help my neighbor, *means*: 'An act of a certain kind will cause something good', and consequently he is here offering a *definition* of the terms 'ought' and 'duty', viz. causing something good. . . .
>
> Yet, if anything is certain, it is that by 'I ought to do so and so' we do not *mean* 'doing so and so will cause something good'.[3]

Thus, according to Prichard, Moore is wrong to define "ought" in terms of "good." And so, the fact remains that we are unjustified in moving from good to ought without providing a link.

Notice also how Prichard's critique of Moore in the above passage is similar to Moore's critique of the naturalists. Just as Moore declared it a fallacy to say that "good" *means* "pleasure," so Prichard is declaring it fallacious to say that "I ought to do so and so" means "doing so and so will cause something good."

In fact, we can reinforce Prichard's case by applying a variant of Moore's open question argument to Moore himself. Suppose "I ought to do so and so" really meant "doing so and so will cause something good." Then saying, "So and so will cause something good, but ought I to do it?" would be equivalent to asking, "So and so will cause something good, but will it cause something good?" But obviously the former question is meaningful and not equivalent to the latter meaningless one.

Even if goodness and obligation are so intimately bound that no separate link is needed, it is a fact that many people, such as Prichard, do not see how they are so bound. Therefore, if Moore's theory is to give a complete and clear account of ultimate justification, the theory should somehow make it clear that goodness and obligation are so intimately related. In other words, since the relation between goodness and obligation is far from obvious, the burden of the proof (that they are so related) is on Moore.[4]

In short, the link between good and ought is still missing; so Moore's theory has failed to give a complete explanation as to why one ought to do a particular act. Accordingly, it will not suffice as an account of ultimate justification.

HOW PRICHARD ACCOUNTS FOR ULTIMATE JUSTIFICATION

The conclusion from the above discussion is that the rightness or obligatoriness of an act cannot be derived from goodness or from anything else. Instead, Prichard claims, rightness or obligation pertains to the act itself. "The word 'ought' refers to actions and to actions alone."[5]

But what is it about an act that makes it right or obligatory? Rightness consists of certain specific relations which vary from one situation to another, for example,

> the obligation to repay a benefit involves a relation due to a past act of the benefactor. . . . On the other hand, the obligation to speak the truth implies no such definite act; it involves a relation consisting in the fact that others are trusting us to speak the truth. . . .the relation involved in an obligation need not be a relation to another at all. Thus we should admit that there is an obligation to overcome our natural timidity or greediness, and that this involves no relations to others. Still there is a relation involved, viz. a relation to our own disposition.[6]

How do we become aware of the rightness of acts—since according to Prichard we cannot do so by a process of inference? As long as we are sufficiently familiar with the facts of a situation, "we appreciate the obligation immediately or directly."[7] In fact, "the sense of obligation to do, or of the rightness of, an action of a particular kind is absolutely underivative or immediate."[8] Thus, for Prichard, our knowledge of obligation is direct and intuitive just as the knowledge of good is for Moore.

History of Justification (Continued)

Furthermore, Prichard declares that such an apprehension of the rightness of an act is a matter of indubitable knowledge. "This apprehension is immediate, in precisely the sense in which a mathematical apprehension is immediate, e.g. the apprehension that this three-sided figure, in virtue of its being three-sided, must have three angles. . . . in both cases the fact apprehended is self-evident."[9] And he also says of our obligations, "This realization of their self-evidence is positive knowledge."[10]

Since, for Prichard, one can have immediate and positive knowledge that he ought to do certain acts, he does not need further justification or reasons for doing them. Therefore, Prichard seems to have demonstrated how acts can have the kind of ultimate justification we have been seeking.

* * *

Incidentally, Prichard has enabled us to clarify further the concept of ultimate justification: For an act to be justified in an absolute sense, it is not sufficient that the goal it aims at be intrinsically good or even that that goal have absolute moral value in Moore's sense. Since in the last analysis ethics has to do with agents' acts, what we are after is an explanation of ultimate justification for those *acts*. An account of ultimate justification must pertain to the act itself; it must show why this very act must be done, not merely why some result is valuable.

AYER'S CRITICISM OF PRICHARD

To see whether our next philosopher, A. J. Ayer (b. 1910), can poke holes in Prichard's account of ultimate justification, we must first sketch Ayer's general critique of naturalism and intuitionism as a whole.

Moore had shown that "good" cannot mean "pleasant" or any other natural or metaphysical property by showing with his open question argument that we do not use "good" synonymously with "pleasant" (or with any other natural or metaphysical property). To quote Moore again: "Whatever definition be offered, it may be always asked, with significance, of the complex so defined, whether it is itself good."[11]

Ayer likewise argues that "good" is not synonymous with terms like "pleasant." But he does not do so by showing that we can with *significance question* whether something acknowledged to be pleasant is good, but by showing that we can *without self-contradiction deny* it:

> Since it is not self-contradictory to say that some pleasant things are not good, or that some bad things are desired, it cannot be the case that the sentence "x is good" is equivalent to "x is pleasant," or to "x is desired." And to every other variant of utilitarianism with which I am acquainted the same objection can be made.[12]

Although Ayer focuses on utilitarianism (and also on what he calls subjectivism), his objections will apply to any other naturalistic or metaphysical theory. And so, in this brief passage, Ayer is accomplishing exactly what Moore accomplished with his open question argument. And Ayer's argument is very similar to Moore's—the main difference being Ayer's reference to denying without contradiction, rather than to questioning without absurdity.

Although this central passage in Ayer's argument is almost the same as Moore's, if we consider the overall context of Ayer's presentation, his argument is fundamentally very different from Moore's. Moore's purpose was merely to refute the claim of naturalists and metaphysicians that good is identical to pleasure or self-realization (or whatever) so that he could go on to establish good as an indefinable quality. Ayer's purpose, however, is much bolder: to prove that all ethical judgments are meaningless.

Ayer's strategy is as follows: Earlier in *Language, Truth and Logic* he had defended the well-known principle of verifiability.[13] This principle says that for a sentence to be meaningful, it must state facts and must be empirically verifiable (unless it is analytic, e.g., a tautology such as "All bachelors are single," in which case it would not provide new knowledge anyway). Thus, if a statement is intended to be informative yet cannot be supported by any evidence, it is meaningless.

It would be beyond the scope of this chapter to review arguments for the verifiability principle, but some examples may make it plausible for the layman. Imagine that a theologian claims that ten angels can dance on the head of a pin. Suppose further that there is no way in the world that we could ever verify whether this claim is true. It would seem to follow that the statement "Ten angels can dance on the head of a pin" is not only unverifiable, but downright meaningless. Because it is hopeless that we can ever know whether it is true, it is useless and absurd to talk about it.

Similarly, *if* there is no way to answer metaphysical questions such as whether people have immortal souls, whether God is omnipotent, whether another universe existed before this universe came into being, and so on, then we are wasting our time discussing and thinking about them. They are meaningless. (Incidentally, whether the questions cited in these examples are verifiable is another matter. Some would argue that the recent extensive testimony of people who have been clinically dead and come back to life does verify that people have immortal souls, and that the statement that people have immortal souls is therefore meaningful.)

As we have seen, Ayer has shown that statements like "This is good" are not equivalent to statements like "This is pleasant," nor to any other statements about natural properties. In other words, he has disposed of the assumption that "statements of ethical value can be translated into statements of empirical fact."[14] Since ethical statements are not factual—nor translatable into factual ones—they cannot be verified. (Obviously a sentence would have to be about facts in order to be verified.) Since judgments about good, right, duty, etc., cannot be verified, they cannot even have meaning.

However, an objection can be raised. According to Ayer and his fellow logical empiricists, statements of empirical fact are counted as meaningful because they are *verifiable*. If we could discover another type of ethical judgment which is verifiable in some non-empirical way, it too should be meaningful. Indeed this is precisely what Moore and Prichard have discovered: that by intuition we can verify that so and so is good, or that such and such is right!

Impossible, says Ayer:

> For it is notorious that what seems intuitively certain to one person may seem doubtful, or even false, to another. So that unless it is possible to provide some criterion by which one may decide between conflicting intuitions, a mere appeal to intuition is worthless as a test of a proposition's validity. But in the case of moral judgements, no such criterion can be

given. Some moralists claim to settle the matter by saying that they "know" that their own moral judgements are correct. But such an assertion is of purely psychological interest, and has not the slightest tendency to prove the validity of any moral judgement. For dissentient moralists may equally well "know" that their ethical views are correct.[15]

If Ayer is right in saying that ethical judgments cannot be verified by intuition, and if he is right in saying that they cannot be translated into empirical statements (by way of naturalism), we must conclude that all ethical judgments are totally meaningless—assuming that the verifiability principle also is correct.

Even if one cannot subscribe to the logical empiricists' verifiability principle and go so far as to call all ethical judgments utterly meaningless, the above passage from Ayer can be a pretty convincing refutation of intuitionism. In other words, Ayer's vivid reminder of how intuitions of good and right can vary among individuals and cultures no doubt immunizes many readers against Prichard's eloquent claim that one's intuition of good or right constitutes positive knowledge.

In a 1949 article, Ayer attempts another refutation of intuitionism which does not rely on the verifiability principle, and which is ironically similar to Moore's and Prichard's refutations. Ayer points out that although the content of the intuitionist's experience may be indefinable, as Moore and Prichard claimed, the experience of such content would be a fact, and the content itself would have to be somewhat distinct and discrete, or else we could not even recognize it and talk about it. Because this content would be something distinct and factual, it would be fallacious for us to presume to identify it with goodness or rightness—just as we are committing a fallacy if we identify any distinct natural or metaphysical property with goodness or rightness.

> Thus even if an intuitionist does have experiences that others do not have, it makes no difference to the argument. We are still entitled to say that it is misleading for him to use a value-term to designate the content of such experiences; for in this way he contrives to smuggle a normative judgement into what purports to be a statement of fact.[16]

And, just as Moore clinches his case by using the open question argument, so Ayer reinforces his with the following reasoning which is very similar to Moore's open question argument.

> I suppose that what underlies it [the dispute about the objectivity of values] is the question: Are the things that I value really valuable, and how can I know that they are? Then one party gives the answer: They are really valuable if they reflect, or participate in. . . . an objective world of values; and you can know that they are by inspecting this world. . . . [But] suppose that someone did succeed in carrying out such an inspection. . . . He can still raise the question: Are these values the real ones? Are the objects that I am inspecting themselves really valuable, and how can I know that they are?[17]

Thus again, even without appealing to the principle of verifiability, Ayer seems to have disposed of intuitionism by means of the same reasoning Moore used to refute naturalism. (And essentially the same logic was used by Prichard to refute Moore, as we noted earlier.)

To conclude, Ayer has undermined Prichard's account of ultimate justification. He has done so by demonstrating the meaninglessness of moral judgments. Or if one rejects the verifiability thesis, Ayer has refuted Prichard

History of Justification (Continued)

by discrediting those intuitions which the intuitionists claimed were the basis of moral judgments. It follows that the justification which Prichard offered is not the ultimate justification we are looking for.

DOES AYER'S EMOTIVISM HELP ACCOUNT FOR JUSTIFICATION?

For Ayer, the only legitimate contents of ethical theory are "propositions which express definitions of ethical terms, or judgements about the legitimacy or possibility of certain definitions."[18] The foregoing sketch of Ayer's views is the kind of discourse he had in mind, for we have been discussing the legitimacy and possibility of various definitions of ethical terms. Since for Ayer all moral judgments are devoid of meaning, it is hardly necessary to state that he made no attempt to explain how one's acts can be morally justified. And so, it is clear that Ayer's emotivism does not help to account for ultimate justification.

A NOTE ON STEVENSON

Although Ayer's critique in *Language, Truth and Logic* seemed to leave little room for ethical theory building, later on he indicated approval of the theory developed by Charles Stevenson (1908–1979).[19] What Stevenson did was to extend by stipulation the use of the word "meaning," so that it would cover the "dynamic function" of certain words.[20] According to this new stipulation, ethical judgments did have a special "emotive meaning."[21] In his book *Ethics and Language* he defines "emotive meaning" this way:

> The emotive meaning of a word is the power that the word acquires, on account of its history in emotional situations, to evoke or directly express attitudes, as distinct from describing or designating them. . . . In virtue of this kind of meaning, ethical judgments alter attitudes.[22]

As Stevenson fills out his theory, he elaborates on how the emotive meaning of an ethical word includes not only its power to express the speaker's attitude, but also its function of *influencing* the hearer. Ayer had mentioned this function of stimulating action,[23] but Stevenson makes much more of it. He says that ethical judgments typically contain two parts: one part describing the speaker's attitudes, and another which is intended to influence the hearer's attitudes. He illustrates this with "working models." For example, "This is good" means approximately "I approve of this; do so as well." And "He ought to do this" is roughly equivalent to "I disapprove of his leaving this undone; do so as well."[24]

Stevenson then proceeds to analyze at length how ethical disputes are carried on and resolved, especially the various ways one party can change the other's attitudes or behavior.[25] His basic point, nevertheless, is that all ethical discourse is a matter of expressing feelings and trying to influence others' attitudes and actions. Thus, for Stevenson as for Ayer, ethics is not a matter of trying to justify behavior by giving reasons which are self-sufficient or ultimate.

Suppose that Mary persuades Bill to run for city council in order to bring pleasure to poor people. What would interest Stevenson is that Mary *persuaded* Bill and how she managed to do so, e.g., whether by informing him about the facts of the case, or by using exhortation to sway his emotions. If a utilitarian like Mill were to declare that Bill's running was justified because it produced pleasure which is good in itself, Stevenson would not be interested. Or, suppose Prichard were to assert that Bill's decision to run was fully justified because his situation involved an obligation which was not based on any further reasons. Stevenson still would not be interested.

Stevenson would agree with Ayer that such assertions by Mill and Prichard are empirically unverifiable (except insofar as they describe the speaker's attitudes) and lack the sort of factual meaning which Mill and Prichard attributed to them. That is to say, Mill and Prichard are merely expressing their own attitudes—or trying to change others' attitudes—about happiness or about Bill's situation. Thus, it seems obvious that Stevenson also makes no attempt to give the kind of account of ultimate justification which we have been seeking. In fact, for Stevenson as for Ayer, the very idea of ethical justification is meaningless.

* * *

Let us suppose that, despite what Ayer and Stevenson have said, it can somehow be shown that moral judgments have more than emotive meaning. Ayer's critical analysis will have helped us fill out our concept of ultimate justification still more. Specifically, if an account of ultimate justification is somehow still possible, it will have to overcome the difficulty Ayer revealed regarding the reliability of people's intuitions of good and right. An account of ultimate justification will have to eliminate any possibility of doubt that the thing which serves as a basis for ultimate justification is indeed a true basis. In other words, an account of ultimate justification must incorporate some proof or guarantee of the authenticity or soundness of the property, principle, or whatever it may be, on which the justification is supposed to be based (i.e., something comparable to the knowledge of authenticity which Prichard claimed for his intuition of rightness, but which Ayer disputed). We can think of this requirement as a further criterion which an account of ultimate justification would have to meet.

THE RISE OF ANALYSIS

The crescendo of criticism of traditional ethical theory which reached its climax in Ayer seemed to prohibit further development of any theories except ones which were essentially emotive, such as the one Stevenson articulated. There no longer seemed to be any possibility at all of ever accounting for the one thing we are primarily concerned about in this book, namely, ultimate justification in ethics.

Of course, philosophers do not give up so easily. Support continued for the naturalistic, the metaphysical, and the intuitionist positions.[26]

Other approaches to ethics which grew in popularity, especially in the late 1940's and 1950's, were existentialism and phenomenology. Existentialism and phenomenology were less susceptible to Ayer's critique and were largely confined to the continent of Europe, where the British empirical tradition and the critiques of Moore, Prichard, Ayer, etc., did not loom so large.

Another alternative to emotivism began developing in England and America after World War II. This new approach to ethics was worked out in the writings of Stephen Toulmin, J. O. Urmson, R. M. Hare, P. H. Nowell-Smith, Kurt Baier, and others.

History of Justification (Continued)

As with Ayer and Stevenson, the method these philosophers used can be described as linguistic analysis or metaethics. The basic message common to all of these later analysts was that Ayer's belief in the meaninglessness of ethical judgments was based on a crucial error—one which had also infected all of the traditional naturalistic, metaphysical, and intuitionist theories. This error was to try to force ethical discourse into a logical model that was inappropriate for it—namely, the logic of science. In the following passage, Nowell-Smith (b. 1914) explains what Ayer and the others were doing that was wrong.

> It was implicitly held that the logic of every type of discourse must be identical. Grammarians might be interested in verbal forms, statements, questions, commands, wishes, and so on. But the province of philosophy was Truth and the sole vehicle of Truth was thought to be the 'proposition', expressed in an indicative sentence which ascribes a 'quality' to an 'object'. Other moods and sentence-forms and other uses to which sentences might be put, however important they might be in other ways, were irrelevant to the quest for Truth.[27]

This slavery to the scientific model stemmed from at least three erroneous assumptions. One was the belief that terms like "good" and "right" must refer to some definite property. Moore had assumed that he was making a great advance when he "discovered" that the property referred to by the word "good" is indefinable. Ayer thought the logical empiricists were making a still greater advance when they revealed that Moore's and Prichard's intuited qualities of good and right are nonexistent, and furthermore that ethical judgments are meaningless. This whole conception of the meaning of "good" and "right" as involving nothing but reference to properties, however, is now discredited by the writings of Toulmin, Hare, Nowell-Smith, and the other new analytic philosophers.

A second erroneous assumption made by Moore, Ayer, and the others was that, insofar as there is a logical structure to ethical discourse, its propositions must be indicative statements like those of science.

The third assumption these thinkers made was that ethical reasoning must either be inductive or have its conclusions inferred from premises by the same strict deductive logic that mathematics uses.

In general, the analysts' rejection of the scientific model for ethics was inspired by Wittgenstein's emphasis in his lectures during the 1930's and 1940's on the *uses* of words rather than on their denotations. As it was stated later in his *Philosophical Investigations*, "For a *large* class of cases—though not for all—in which we employ the word 'meaning' it can be defined thus: the meaning of a word is its use in the language."[28]

Following Wittgenstein, the analysts stopped trying to define ethical terms. Instead, they began investigating the various jobs ethical words do in actual discourse, and the different functions of ethical statements. Although they did not always agree on exactly how multifarious these jobs and functions can become, the new emphasis on uses rather than definition is expressed nicely in the following paragraph by Nowell-Smith:

> The old model is not just misleading; it is wholly wrong. The words with which moral philosophers have especially to do, which are usually called 'value-words', play many different parts. They are used to express tastes and preferences, to express decisions and choices, to criticize, grade, and evaluate, to advise, admonish, warn, persuade and dissuade, to

praise, encourage and reprove, to promulgate and draw attention to rules; and doubtless for other purposes also. These activities form the complex web of moral discourse and our problem is to trace the connections between them and to come to understand how it is that the same word can be used in all these different ways. What a man is doing with a particular value-word at a particular time can only be discovered by examining what he says in its context. . .[29]

By merely mapping out the various functions of ethical expressions, can these philosophers provide what we are looking for—an account of ultimate justification? It is difficult to give a general answer. Nowell-Smith, for one, implies that to account for ultimate justification would take one outside the province of ethics.[30] And in Chapter 5, we will begin an attempt to find out whether Hare can give such an account.

But one of these disciples of Wittgenstein who makes an obvious effort to account for ultimate justification is Toulmin. Since his writing on this point is unusually explicit, he will be the last philosopher in our historical survey before we turn to Hare.

NOTES

[1] H. A. Prichard, "Does Moral Philosophy Rest on a Mistake?" *Mind*, 21, no. 81, Jan. 1912, reprinted in Prichard, *Moral Obligation* (Oxford: Oxford University Press, 1968), p. 4. In this passage Prichard goes on to add, "An 'ought,' if it is to be derived at all, can only be derived from another 'ought'."

[2] Moore, Sect. 89, p. 146.

[3] H. A. Prichard, *Moral Obligation* (Oxford: Oxford University Press, 1968), p. 145. This passage is from Prichard's unfinished book *Moral Obligation*, whose title is also used for this collection of his works on ethics.

[4] As Prichard points out on page 146 of *Moral Obligation*, later on when Moore was writing his *Ethics* (1912), he seemed to acknowledge that he had identified good and obligation too closely in *Principia*. That is, in 1912 Moore seemed to modify his stand so that it was closer to Prichard's. See Moore, *Ethics* (London: Oxford University Press, 1947), p. 107.

[5] Prichard, "Does Moral Philosophy Rest on a Mistake?" in the volume *Moral Obligation*, p. 4.

[6] *Ibid.*, p. 8. In his British Academy lecture of 1932, "Duty and Ignorance of Fact" (in the volume *Moral Obligation*, p. 18) Prichard in a sense modified or at least expanded upon his views on this point. In this lecture, he debates the question, "If a man has an obligation, i.e. a duty, to do some action, does the obligation depend on certain characteristics of the situation in which he is, or on certain characteristics of his thought about the situation?" (p. 18). Prichard's conclusion is in favor of the second alternative, which he calls the subjective view. On the other hand, in "Does Moral Philosophy Rest on a Mistake?" he had carefully formulated his view this way: "The rightness of an action consists in its being the origination of something of a certain kind A in a situation of a certain kind, a situation consisting in a certain relation B of the agent to others or to his own nature" (p. 7), which is closer to the first alternative quoted above. Thus, in later years, he came to think of obligation as grounded in a more complex relationship—one which has more to do with the *thoughts* of the agent.

[7] *Ibid.*, p. 8.
[8] *Ibid.*, p. 7.
[9] *Ibid.*, p. 8.
[10] *Ibid.*, p. 16.
[11] Moore, *Principia*, p. 15.
[12] A. J. Ayer, *Language, Truth and Logic* (New York: Dover Publications, Inc., 1952), p. 105.
[13] *Ibid.*, pp. 35–41.
[14] *Ibid.*, p. 104.
[15] *Ibid.*, p. 106.
[16] A. J. Ayer, "On the Analysis of Moral Judgements," *Horizon*, 20, no. 117 (1949), 178–179.
[17] *Ibid.*, p. 179.
[18] Ayer, *Language, Truth and Logic*, p. 103.

[19] *Ibid.*, p. 20. See also "On the Analysis of Moral Judgements," p. 176.

[20] Cf. C. L. Stevenson, "The Emotive Meaning of Ethical Terms," *Mind*, 46 (1938), 21–23.

[21] Cf. C. K. Ogden and I. A. Richards, *The Meaning of Meaning* (London: Kegan Paul, 1923) for an early use of the word "emotive," p. 125.

[22] C. L. Stevenson, *Ethics and Language* (New Haven: Yale University Press, 1944), p. 33.

[23] Ayer, *Language, Truth and Logic*, p. 108.

[24] Stevenson, *Ethics and Language*, p. 21.

[25] *Ibid.*, p. 115 ff.

[26] For example, Perry continued to uphold the naturalistic view. For his defense of a rather subjective form of naturalism vis-a-vis Ayer, see R. B. Perry, *Realms of Value* (Cambridge, Mass.: Harvard University Press, 1954), pp. 7–9, 120. Ross, the most prominent proponent of deontological intuitionism after Prichard, published his second major work on ethics three years after the appearance of Ayer's book. For his detailed rejoinder to Ayer, see W. D. Ross, *Foundations of Ethics* (Oxford: The Clarendon Press, 1939), pp. 34–41.

[27] P. H. Nowell-Smith, *Ethics* (Harmondsworth: Penguin Books, Ltd., 1954), p. 21.

[28] Ludwig Wittgenstein, *Philosophical Investigations* (Oxford: Basil Blackwell, 2nd Edition, 1958), section 43.

[29] Nowell-Smith, p. 98.

[30] Cf. *Ibid.*, pp. 319–320.

III

Toulmin: Social Harmony As The Basis of Justification

TOULMIN'S ATTACK ON THE EARLIER THEORIES

Stephen E. Toulmin (b. 1922) studied under Wittgenstein (1889–1951) at Cambridge, and his book, *The Place of Reason in Ethics*, was the first major work on ethics to make extensive use of Wittgenstein's insights.[1] The first quarter of the book consists of criticisms of others' theories, including intuitionism and emotivism. Toulmin goes along with the other analysts who deny (1) that ethical words must refer to properties, (2) that ethical statements must be indicative or descriptive propositions, and (3) that the logic of moral reasoning must be inductive or deductive.

Like other followers of Wittgenstein, Toulmin advises us to observe how actual ethical discourse works. Because the intuitionists had assumed that all adjectives, including ethical ones, must refer to properties, they inferred that when talking ethics, we must be trying to find out what acts have the property of rightness, or what results have the quality good, and so on. But, says Toulmin, if we examine what we are actually doing when engaging in ethical talk, we will notice that we are seeking *reasons* to guide our decisions.

Notice what we do when confronted with a significant moral decision, e.g., whether to take the orphan next door to visit the zoo. Deliberation over such a decision does not normally consist of searching for some property of goodness or rightness inhering in the act. Rather, to come to a decision about this, one would weigh the reasons for making the visit (reasons such as how the orphan would enjoy the visit) against the reasons for not making it (e.g., the need to finish work in the office).[2]

Toulmin sums up this observation as follows:

> 'Rightness' is not a property; and when I asked the two people which course of action was the right one I was not asking them about a property—what I wanted to know was whether there was any reason for choosing one course of action rather than another....
>
> Finally, this reconstruction explains why those philosophers who are attracted to the objective approach [i.e. intuitionism] pay so little attention to what we regard as the central question—the place of reason in ethics. In adopting the objective approach (so as to 'preserve the possibility of contradiction' in ethics) they say, in effect: 'Reasons are not enough. Ethical predicates must correspond to ethical properties, and "knowing-what-goodness-is" means recognizing the presence of such a property.' The objective doctrine is, therefore, not just unhelpful to us: it is a positive hindrance, diverting on to arguments about a purely imaginary 'property' the attention which should be paid to the question of ethical reasoning.[3]

Not only intuitionism, but Ayer's emotivism as well, gets criticized by Toulmin: Ayer believed that only indicative statements have meaning, and that all reasoning is deductive or inductive; and therefore he construed the function of all moral discourse as merely the expression of feelings and the influencing of others. But, like naturalists and intuitionists, Ayer was failing to observe how we actually use moral language.

Suppose two neighbors are debating about whether it was right of Mrs. Jones to divorce her husband. They might have a shouting match in which they let out their feelings: "Divorce is wrong!" "He drove her to it!" etc. Such a confrontation would hardly be called moral discourse or discussion. On the other hand, if they do engage in what we normally call moral discourse, they will begin talking about reasons—what good reasons she had for resorting to divorce, reasons why she should have given the marriage another try, religious reasons for or against divorce, and so on. Thus, Ayer's denial of the importance of reason-seeking gives a misleading picture of moral discourse.

These reactions to emotivism are recapitulated by Toulmin as follows:

> Sometimes, when we make ethical judgements, we are not just ejaculating. When we say that so-and-so is good, or that I ought to do such-and-such, we do so sometimes for good reasons and sometimes for bad ones. The imperative approach [Toulmin's name for emotivism] does not help us in the slightest to distinguish the one from the other—in fact, by saying that to talk of reasons in this context is nonsense, it dismisses our question altogether.[4]

Thus, it becomes apparent how, by focusing on the use of language and the role of reasons, Toulmin has undermined not only the more conventional moralists like Moore and Prichard, but even the one whose critical and tough-minded skepticism seemed unassailable, namely, Ayer.

TOULMIN'S FRESH APPROACH TO THE PROBLEM OF JUSTIFICATION

Since observation and analysis of the nature of ethical discourse shows that the individual who is busy making a decision is primarily concerned about reasons for choosing one alternative over another, the question immediately arises, What constitutes a valid or good reason?

Toulmin first reminds us of the obvious point that a particular reason is not a good reason merely because someone happens to accept it. To be good, a reason must be *worthy* of acceptance.[5] Secondly, we must notice that what renders a reason worthy of acceptance varies from one situation to another.

In some situations, to show that a proposition *corresponds* to a fact is to give a good reason for accepting the proposition as true. In doing this, one is employing the correspondence theory of truth. However, such use of the correspondence theory holds only for situations involving descriptive propositions.[6] There are plenty of other contexts in which we speak of good reasons without having in mind descriptions and correspondence with facts. For example, Toulmin points out that it is perfectly meaningful.

> to talk of 'good and bad reasons' and of 'valid and invalid inferences' ... in ethics, in aesthetics, in expressing our reactions to things, in explaining our motives, in giving commands, and in our thousand-and-one other ways of using speech! And since, when we employ many of these modes of reasoning, it would be far-fetched to say that we were 'describing' anything, it is not to be expected that the logical criteria appropriate to these modes will be those relevant to descriptions. Rather, we must expect that every mode of

reasoning, every type of sentence, and (if one is particular) every single sentence will have its own logical criteria, to be discovered by examining its individual, peculiar uses.[7]

Toulmin is asserting that what makes a reason worthy of acceptance depends on the context. He is arguing that naturalists, intuitionists, and emotivists have made a mistake in putting such emphasis on description and correspondence to facts. That is, they have erred by assuming that when giving a reason for doing an act, one must be describing something, e.g., one's response as pleasurable, a result as good, or the act as right.[8]

Rather, in judging whether an *ethical* reason is good or valid, we use criteria which are different from those relevant to descriptions. But Toulmin has not yet told us what those peculiarly ethical criteria are. He has yet to explain what, in the realm of ethics, renders a reason a good reason.

REASONS IN SCIENCE

First Toulmin finds that an examination of scientific reasoning will make it easier to understand how reasons function in ethics. To start with an example Toulmin gives:

If, from a pile of brushwood, we pick out those branches that look straightest, we shall, as a matter of fact, make the same selection as we should if we picked out those which feel straightest, or compared their lengths with the distances between their ends, or sighted along them.[9]

In this case, any of the techniques mentioned—looking, feeling, etc.—will yield a description of the sticks (e.g., "this stick is the straightest") which corresponds to the facts (e.g., that this is in fact the straightest stick). Thus, in a simple situation, description and correspondence to fact provide an adequate basis for reasoning about the straightness of sticks.

On the other hand, in more complex situations it is often inappropriate to base one's reasoning on simple descriptions and correspondence to facts. Citing another of Toulmin's examples,

> if we are standing around [a stick half submerged in water], and each gives his own account of how it looks to him, we shall differ in what we say. Some will say, 'It's bent to the left'; others, 'It's bent to the right'; and one or two, 'It's just foreshortened'.[10]

In this case, a mere description of what we observe will not necessarily enlighten us about the facts regarding the straightness of the stick. Thus, in situations like this, simple description and the correspondence theory are inadequate.

To give an adequate reason or explanation of such puzzling phenomena, a different kind of reasoning is required, which Toulmin illustrates as follows:

> . . . to satisfy your demand for an 'explanation' . . . I can show you that this is something that always happens in such circumstances; that it is not a peculiarity of this particular stick or this particular stream, but that any straight piece of wood, metal or other solid, plunged into any smooth, level stretch of water, in stream or pond, in tank or wash-basin, looks the same. . . .
>
> All these things will help to make the phenomenon seem less surprising. All of them will help to satisfy your demand for an 'explanation'. All of them do so by giving an explanation of the same kind, an explanation taken from *physics*, the appropriate

science. And each explanation is designed to show that, from our experience of optical phenomena, the bending of the stick was 'to be expected'."[11]

This passage is an example of the way Toulmin, without employing the technical jargon of pragmatism, operationism, and so on, goes to great lengths to show that in the bent stick case and in other cases dealt with by science, finding adequate reasons really amounts to discovering what is to be *expected*. That is, in situations where we employ science, what we are seeking is a set of reasons (a theory) which will enable us to make reliable predictions. Therefore, in this sort of situation, a reason will be *good* by virtue of its performing that role, i.e., helping us predict. As he puts it briefly, "the question, 'What is the explanation of this?', has the same force as, 'How would a physicist have come to predict this?' "[12]

The general point Toulmin is trying to illustrate by discussing science is that the kinds of reasons which are worthy of acceptance vary from situation to situation, and that a reason is good by virtue of its accomplishing what it is intended to accomplish in the situation. In everyday situations like judging which stick in a pile is the straightest, our reasoning has the function of describing facts; but in science good reasons are those which enable us to predict. Toulmin sums up this insight:

> The question, what makes a reason a 'good' reason in science, and what makes an argument or explanation a 'valid' one, can only be answered in terms of the reasons, arguments and explanations we *do* accept—namely, those which are predictively reliable, coherent and convenient. If we give up these criteria for others, we change the nature of our activity and, whatever we are now doing, it is no longer 'science'. The logical criteria applicable to scientific explanations are, in this

respect, quite as intimately connected with the nature of the activity which we *call* 'science' as the logic and the activity of 'describing things'. . . .[13]

REASONS IN ETHICS

To apply to ethics the insight we have gained from our detour into science—that reasons are worthy of acceptance by virtue of their performing the function they are intended to perform—let us now investigate the function of reasons in ethics. In ethics the purpose of giving reasons is not to describe, as the intuitionists and others believed it was. Nor is it to predict phenomena as in science. What then is the place of reasons in ethics?

It is important to follow Toulmin's presentation closely on this point.[14] Suppose two people are arguing about what to do, and they finally agree on a certain course of action. "What kinds of reasons would they have to bring for and against [the acts in question] . . . in order for us to say that 'ethical' considerations had affected their decisions. . .?"[15] One answer might be given that a reason was ethical if it had to do with promoting harmony and avoiding suffering in the community. However, many would protest that considerations of suffering, pleasure, etc., ignore the most important aspect of ethics, namely, duty.

In reply to this objection, Toulmin (true to the analytic approach) suggests that we examine how ethical reasoning is actually carried on. Suppose we are observing the members of a totally unfamiliar culture and are trying to find out what they consider to be duties. We probably would not *ask* them outright, because translating from their language into ours would be risky, and because they might not even have a word corresponding to our word "duty." It would be safer to *observe* their behavior.

Would we observe which behavior they rewarded and punished? No. Doing this exclusively could be misleading, since we often reward non-moral behavior such as good manners and the wearing of nice clothes. Suppose that "winning competitions or wearing the right-colored trousers" were rewarded, or failing to do so were punished, while they "let murder and rape, robbery and lying go by unnoticed."[16] Would we conclude that this society considered the latter acts ethically acceptable? Indeed not. In fact, Toulmin points out, we would hardly even call this group a community!

Three passages will now be quoted which follow closely within two pages. These passages are the key to Toulmin's whole theory, so especially close attention should be paid to them. In referring to the fact that the term "community" would not be used for a group which let murder, lying, etc., go by unnoticed, Toulmin explains more fully that a collection of people is called a community only if the members respect one another's interests.

> This fact is most important: it shows us the nature of . . . our concept of 'duty', too. For consider what kinds of thing we require before we agree to call any collection of people a 'community'. Suppose, for example, that we visit an island, and find that its inhabitants all habitually avoid types of behavior particularly liable to inconvenience their fellows: then we shall be prepared to refer to the inhabitants of the island as forming a single 'community'. And we shall also say that the members of the community 'recognize a duty to one another', and 'have a moral code'. But if, instead, we find that we have to divide the inhabitants into two classes, C_1 and C_2—such that members of C_1 are scrupulous only insofar as their

conduct affects other members of C_1, but ignore the interests of those of C_2; and those of C_2 respect the interests of other members of C_2, but ignore those of C_1—we shall not be able to call them 'members of a single community' at all. In fact, we shall call the two sets of people, C_1 and C_2, 'separate communities'. Likewise, we shall not be able to say that members of C_1 'recognize any duty' to members of C_2 or vice versa.[17]

In the foregoing passage, Toulmin has pointed out that members of a community necessarily recognize a duty to one another. Now he will explain that saying they do so is a truism, because a community is defined as a group in which members respect one another's interests:

The 'anthropological discovery' that 'all communities recognize the Absolute Value of Duty' is therefore not a discovery at all, but something which an anthropologist could safely announce before he ever set out: it only explains, in an obscure and roundabout way, part of what we mean by the notion of a 'community'. 'In all "communities" (i.e. groups of people living together, and respecting one another's interests)', our informant is saying, in effect, 'people control their behavior so as to have regard for one another's interests'. His 'law of human nature' is a truism.[18]

Toulmin will finally sum up the point he has been driving at by laying bare the origin and essence of the concept of duty. Since a group is a community only if members respect one another's interests, the concept of duty is necessarily present; duty and respect for the interests of others cannot be separated. That is, the very function of the term "duty" (and also of "ethics") is to maintain the community by harmonizing the desires of the members. (Thus, the so-called deontological, or duty oriented, and teleological, or goal oriented, aspects of the concept of duty are inseparable.)

The concept of 'duty', in short, is inextricable from the 'mechanics' of social life, and from the practices adopted by different communities in order to make living together in proximity tolerable or even possible. We need not therefore worry about the apparent duality of ethical arguments—about the contrast between arguments from 'duty' and arguments from the welfare of our fellows. And we can fairly characterise ethics as a part of the process whereby the desires and actions of the members of a community are harmonised.[19]

Toulmin is not merely giving the stock naturalistic argument (e.g., of Mill and Perry) that duty, right, etc., can be derived from considerations of desire, pleasure, satisfaction, and so on. Instead, he claims to be doing something basically different. He is saying that just as in science the very purpose or function of reasoning is to help us predict phenomena, so *the very function* of reasoning about duty and ethical behavior is to harmonize desires within the community.

Nevertheless, one may object that Toulmin still seems to be identifying the harmonizing of desires with good (à la naturalism)[20] or to be asserting that harmonizing desires *has* goodness (as an intuitionist might).

If Toulmin were doing either of these two things, he would be construing ethical sentences as descriptive or as indicative of properties. But Toulmin has renounced such a wild goose chase after ethical properties, as we have seen. Rather, when he observes that talk about duty, good, and right has the function of harmonizing people's desires, he is not asserting that it is good or right to harmonize desires. He is simply doing the former, i.e., *observing* that ethical talk *has the function* of harmonizing desires.

If harmonizing desires truly is the function of ethical reasoning, it will follow that acceptable ethical reasoning is that which performs the function of harmonizing desires. Thus, without lapsing into naturalism or intuitionism, but by resolutely *observing* the *uses* of language in ethics, Toulmin seems to have demonstrated what kind of ethical reasons are worthy of acceptance.

We must conclude, then, that as long as reasons for a particular *act* are acceptable in the way we have indicated, the act will be morally *justified*.[21]

ULTIMATE JUSTIFICATION

Now we can turn to the orignal question: How does Toulmin account for ultimate justification? He has shown that in ethics reasons which perform the function of harmonizing desires are worthy of acceptance. Or to use our earlier terminology, they are "justified." But are they justified in the ultimate sense we have been concerned about? Are these reasons self-sufficient and independent of any further justification? Is it appropriate to ask *why* reasons which perform their function of harmonizing desires are worthy of acceptance?

Toulmin emphatically answers, No. And he takes many pages in various parts of the second half of his book to present the insight that indeed further justification is unnecessary. First, he again uses the parallel with science to help make this point. In a section titled "The 'Justification' of Science" he argues that although we can appeal to the logic of science to justify particular scientific explanations, it is inappropriate to ask for a justification of scientific explanations in general:

> Indeed, so natural and inevitable does the logic of science come to appear that one cannot help being a little taken aback,

when a philosopher comes along and asks us how we justify, not just a particular one, but *all* scientific explanations. For, apart from a more detailed and accurate account than I have had room to give of the way in which science develops—an account which could only be of use to us in justifying *this* explanation, as opposed to *that* one, and not 'explanations in general'—what kind of answer can be needed?

It is clear from the start that there is no room *within* science for the philosopher's inquiry.[22]

He asserts that something similar must be said about the request for further justification of our reasoning in ethics. In a section titled "Is any 'Justification' of Ethics Needed?" he says:

I myself do not feel the need for any *general* answer to the question, 'What makes some ethical reasoning "good" and some ethical arguments "valid"?': answers applicable to particular types of argument are enough. In fact, it seems to me that the demand for any such general answer (however it is to be obtained) must lead one to paradox as surely as did the corresponding demand over science.[23]

Later in this same passage, he again asserts that there is no need for further justification for "all reasoning about conduct" (by which he means reasoning which functions to harmonize desires) nor for "ethics as a whole" (i.e., the enterprise of harmonizing desires):

Ethics may be able to 'justify' one of a number of courses of action, or one social practice as opposed to another: but it does not extend to the 'justification' of all reasoning about conduct. One course of action can be opposed to another: one social practice can be opposed to another. But to what are we expected to oppose 'ethics-as-a-whole'? . . . and, if those who call for a 'justification' of ethics want 'the case for morality', as opposed to 'the case for expediency', etc., then they are giving philosophy a job which is not its own.[24]

Although Toulmin is anything but concise as he keeps coming back to his case about justification, the logic of his overall argument can (without oversimplification) be summarized in the following steps:

1. The attempt to find the meaning of ethical words by searching for properties proved futile. Instead, observation and analysis show that ethical discourse has to do with finding *reasons* for one's acts or for social practices.
2. The kinds of reasons which are worthy of acceptance vary from situation to situation. But we can lay down the general rule that reasons are worthy of acceptance in any situation insofar as they perform the function intended for them.
3. The basic function of ethical reasons is to harmonize desires within the community—as we have discovered from our observation of the use of ethical language.
4. Therefore, the reasons which are worthy of acceptance in ethics will be those which perform the function of harmonizing desires within the community.
5. We can conclude that particular *acts* are *justified* morally to the extent that the reasons for doing them are worthy of acceptance in this sense (i.e., of harmonizing desires).
6. Does this overall institution itself need to be justified—i.e., the institution of justifying acts by giving reasons in terms of harmonizing desires within the community? Of course not. Our observation and

analysis of the uses of ethical language have made clear that in ethical contexts the sole function of the word "justify" is to give reasons in terms of harmonizing desires for *particular* acts or practices. Therefore, it is obviously inappropriate to try to apply the term "justify" to the institution within which the justifying of particular acts is carried on.

If someone is still skeptical about Toulmin's doctrine, he should be reminded that it was by observing the functioning of ethical discourse that we discovered justification to be a matter of giving reasons for acts in terms of harmonizing desires. The only additional argument we need to offer is to say, "Check for yourself whether our observations and analyses have been accurate."

To conclude, particular acts are justified insofar as they are given reasons in terms of harmonizing desires. Since no further ethical justification can or need be asked for, it would seem as if Toulmin has accounted for justification which can be called ultimate.

NOTES

[1] S. E. Toulmin, *The Place of Reason in Ethics* (Cambridge: Cambridge University Press, paperback edition 1960); original edition published in 1950. The only other writing published as early as 1950 which had comparable influence among the contemporary analytic moralists was Urmson's article, "On Grading," *Mind*, 59 (1950).

[2] This and the next example are my own, not Toulmin's.
[3] Toulmin, p. 28.
[4] *Ibid.*, p. 60.
[5] *Ibid.*, pp. 70–72.
[6] *Ibid.*, p. 77.

[7] *Ibid.*, p. 83.

[8] For further discussion of his view that logical criteria vary from situation to situation, see Toulmin's book, *The Uses of Argument* (Cambridge: Cambridge University Press, 1958), pp. 174–5, 220–23, 232–35.

[9] Toulmin, *The Place of Reason in Ethics*, p. 90.

[10] *Ibid.*, p. 86.

[11] *Ibid.*, pp. 87–88.

[12] *Ibid.*, p. 96. Cf. p. 95: "In deciding what scientific theory to adopt.... The initial, and most important test is that of *predictive reliability*: the theory must show us that all the observations we have made in the relevant field of study were such as might have been expected, and it must give us the power to predict correctly future observations in the same field." He also points out that if two theories predict equally well, we choose between them on the basis of coherence and convenience. But for our purposes it is not essential to discuss these distinctions. Cf. pp. 95 and 97.

[13] *Ibid.*, p. 101.

[14] *Ibid.*, pp. 132–137.

[15] *Ibid.*, p. 132.

[16] *Ibid.*, p. 134.

[17] *Ibid.*, pp. 134–135.

[18] *Ibid.*, p. 135.

[19] *Ibid.*, p. 136.

[20] For example, C. D. Broad took Toulmin's theory to be a form of hedonistic utilitarianism. Cf. C. D. Broad, "Review of Toulmin: *An Examination of the Place of Reason in Ethics*, *Mind*, 61 (1952), pp. 93–94.

[21] Toulmin also argues that often the justification for an act is that it conforms to the accepted practices of the community. Although he emphasizes this point in certain places in his book (see pp. 144–146), to elaborate on this phase of his doctrine would distract us from our main concern, because this principle—that many acts are justified in terms of accepted practices—is based on the more fundamental one that justification is ultimately a matter of giving reasons in terms of harmonizing desires. Thus, I am centering my discussion around the latter principle because my purpose is not primarily to try to present a balanced picture of his theory, but to articulate his most essential insights regarding ultimate justification.

[22] *Ibid.*, p. 99.
[23] *Ibid.*, p. 161.
[24] *Ibid.*, p. 162.

IV

Toulmin (Continued): Challenges From Hare

THE NATURE OF COMMUNAL LIFE AS AN OBJECTIVE BASIS FOR JUSTIFICATION

Can we challenge Toulmin's account of justification by questioning his methodology? Is the observation and analysis of the way ethical language functions really the highest court of appeal? Witness the reaction of R. M. Hare (b. 1919) to the Toulminian approach in his review of Toulmin's book:

> [According to Toulmin] in order to discover how, by reason, to answer questions of the form 'Which of these courses of action shall I choose?', we first discover what ethics is, by seeing how the word is used; to discover what ethics is, is at the same time to discover what its function is; to discover what its function is, is at the same time to discover what are good reasons in ethics. . . . Thus our moral decisions are to be made, according to this suggestion, on the basis (given knowledge of the material circumstances) of nothing else but our observation of the current usage of the word 'ethical'.
> This advice is so odd that I can scarcely believe that it is what Mr. Toulmin intends.[1]

Thus Hare is doubting Toulmin's basic thesis that we can find out what constitutes justification or good reasons in ethics by observing the functioning of ethical discourse.

It should be noted that Hare seems to be interpreting Toulmin as saying that the purpose of ethical reasoning is whatever purpose the individuals in a community feel at the time—as if the function of ethical language and reasoning would vary from one community or period to another according to people's whims.

Hare is not alone in interpreting Toulmin this way,[2] and Toulmin does seem to invite such an interpretation. When Toulmin was comparing ethical reasoning to science, he said, "The question, what makes a reason a 'good' reason in science, and what makes an argument or explanation a 'valid' one, can only be answered in terms of the reasons, arguments and explanations we *do* accept."[3]

If Toulmin is indeed conceiving of the function of ethical reasoning as being a matter of reasons people do accept and as a matter of whatever happens to be current usage, and if he means this in the superficial way that Hare suggests, Toulmin is leaving himself open to criticisms along these lines: "How can what people currently accept as good reasons in ethics be a firm basis for what *are* good reasons? If some eccentric individual uses 'good' and 'ought' differently from most people, then won't the reasons the eccentric accepts be as worthy as the reasons others accept? Isn't such a foundation for ethics extremely subjective, or even dependent on people's whims?"

It is hard to believe that Toulmin's thesis is so simplistic. It seems that Hare must be missing Toulmin's point here. When Toulmin speaks of the "purpose" or "function" of ethical reasoning, he surely does not mean merely any purpose which people *happen* to have in mind at the time, i.e., something approaching a whim. That is to say, Hare notwithstanding, Toulmin is not conceiving of an arbitrary or subjective acceptance when he speaks of "what reasons people do accept." Rather, he believes that his observation of use reveals what function ethical reasoning *must* have.

I say "must" because there is plenty of evidence in Toulmin's book that he conceives of that function as objective and discoverable through observation, rather than as something which depends on people's temporary feelings or attitudes. It is as if that function were objectively grounded in the very nature of human life and language. In fact, in the three long passages which I call the key to his theory and quoted in the last chapter, Toulmin was explaining how a group of people can be called a community only insofar as they cooperate to harmonize desires. And he concluded that section by saying that "the concept of 'duty', in short, is inextricable from the 'mechanics' of social life, and from the practices adopted by different communities in order to make living together in proximity tolerable or even possible."[4]

Obviously, his point in this key section is that the goal of harmonizing desires is something which human beings *cannot* avoid if they are to live in communities. "But do we have to live in communities?" someone might ask. Perhaps not. But no doubt Toulmin would reply that without community life there would be no duty or ethics in the first place: "The only context in which the concept of 'duty' is straightforwardly intelligible is one of communal life."[5]

Thus, ethical concepts make sense only with respect to life in communities, according to Toulmin. Where a community exists, those ethical concepts must be viewed in terms of harmonizing desires. This is not because people want to harmonize desires, but because it is the very nature of a community that its members *will* cooperate to do so. Again, if a group doesn't cooperate to harmonize desires, it is not even a community.

To clinch his thesis, Toulmin asks us to imagine some people setting out to disprove it:

> Even if 5000 supporters of the 'imperative doctrine'—all of them so enlightened as to realize the 'irrational' nature of morality, and all of them vowing to renounce ethical words and arguments as 'mere rationalisation'—even if they tried to live together as a community, they would soon have to adopt rules of behaviour; and, when it came to educating their children, some of their words would perforce become 'ethical'. 'You'll *burn* yourself if you play with fire', uttered as the child was pulled away from it, would acquire the meaning of our own, 'You *mustn't* play with fire, or you'll *harm* yourself'; 'It's *annoying* of you to cut holes in Daddy's trousers', accompanied by the removal of trousers and scissors, would come to mean, 'It's *naughty* of you to cut holes in Daddy's trousers'; and so on. And, after 20 years, either their 'community' would have ceased to exist, or it would have developed a code as 'moral' as any other—and the fact that the familiar words, 'good', 'bad', 'wicked' and 'virtuous', had been given up would be irrelevant. This sort of thing does happen (I am told) in 'progressive schools', whose products grow up using words like 'cooperative', 'undesirable' and 'anti-social', with all the rhetorical force and emotional associations commonly belonging to 'good', 'wrong' and 'wicked'.[6]

Thus, it is inevitable that members of a community cooperate to harmonize desires, and it is inevitable that their language and reasoning function to further this end. Since this purpose or function of discourse and reasoning is inescapable, we cannot avoid using some words to perform that function. Similarly, we cannot avoid accepting as worthy the reasoning which furthers that end, i.e., reasoning in terms of harmonizing desires. Therefore, such uses and functions are not arbitrary or subjective matters; they are grounded in objective features of human life.

To conclude, when describing the ultimate foundation of his system, we are selling Toulmin short if we emphasize phrases such as "current usage," as Hare did in his review. Such emphasis implies that for Toulmin the basic patterns of ethical language and reasoning, i.e., the foundations of morality, can vary, if not with people's attitudes, then at least from one culture or historical epoch to another. If this were Toulmin's intent, he would be providing an obviously arbitrary basis for ethics. On the other hand, since Toulmin clearly conceives of the fundamental uses of ethical language and reasoning as invariable and grounded in immutable features of community life, he has provided a much firmer basis for moral justification.

HARE'S ARGUMENT THAT TOULMIN CANNOT DERIVE OBLIGATION FROM FACTS

Is this basis for justification so firm that it is beyond further questioning? Is the justification Toulmin has accounted for truly ultimate? Let's take a fresh look at Toulmin's reasoning, and consider another objection by R. M. Hare which goes beyond the one we have just discussed.

Thanks to his emphasis on the uses of language, Toulmin has avoided the mistake of thinking of goodness, rightness, and obligation as properties. Nevertheless Toulmin believes he has derived moral judgments from facts. From various factual considerations—e.g., the fact that Mrs. Jones' getting a divorce will bring peace to everyone—Toulmin claims that we can derive moral or evaluative conclusions, such as that Mrs. Jones *ought* to get a divorce. Toulmin expresses this general viewpoint as follows:

> The evidence of science remains evidence about what is practicable, and so about facts—what *is* or *could be*, not what *ought to be*. It is in the hands of the moralist that possibility becomes policy, what *can* be done becomes what *ought* to be done. All his experience and wisdom are needed to bridge the gap between facts and values. But the gap can be bridged.[7]

To use the jargon, Toulmin is claiming that an "ought" sentence can be derived from an "is" sentence. But Hume and others—including Hare—have declared that it is impossible to bridge the gap from an "ought" to an "is." According to them, the conclusion of a deduction can contain nothing which is not at least implicitly contained in the premises.[8] Therefore, if the conclusion of a chain of moral reasoning is to contain an "ought," the premises must also contain an "ought."

Toulmin, on the contrary, defends his view that moral conclusions *can* be derived from factual considerations by asserting that the rule "Nothing in the conclusion that is not already contained in the premises" applies only to a few disciplines such as mathematics. In other areas such as ethics, a looser kind of inference is in order. As noted earlier, for Toulmin, logical criteria vary from one context to another. In simple situations like picking sticks from a pile, reasons in terms of description of facts will do; in more complex situations, science has to give reasons in terms of prediction. In ethics, the reasons which are worthy of acceptance are those which are in terms of harmonizing desires.

Toulmin (Continued): Challenges From Hare

Therefore, a moral conclusion can be justified if one gives reasons in terms of harmonizing desires. Such reasons normally would be factual statements having to do with peace, pleasure, desires, satisfaction, and so on. Thus, factual statements, or "is" sentences, can justify non-factual "ought" sentences.[9]

Toulmin is not alone in taking this stand. As we pointed out at the beginning of the section on the contemporary analysts, many of these analysts, for example, Nowell-Smith, disagree with the more traditional thinkers (including Ayer) on at least three points, one of which is that the logic of ethical reasoning must be inductive or deductive.

Hare, however, is one analytic philosopher who is strenuously opposed to such a view. In his review of Toulmin's book, and also in *The Language of Morals*, he tries to undercut Toulmin's stand.[10]

In the review, Hare asks us to consider two sentences: first the "is" sentence "This practice would involve the least conflict of interests attainable under the circumstances"; and then the moral judgment "This would be the right practice."[11] According to Toulmin, the first statement is a good reason for the second: Thanks to the logical criterion used in ethics (harmonizing desires), the first sentence implies the second, says Toulmin—although, admittedly, there is not the strict logical entailment which Hume, Hare, and others would insist upon.

But imagine, Hare suggests, that someone else were disputing this by saying, "Without conflict, the full development of manhood is impossible; therefore it is a bad reason for calling a practice right to say that it would involve the least conflict of interests."[12]

Toulmin would claim that this proponent of manhood

was simply wrong in his observation of the uses and function of ethical words. He would say that if we observe the meaning (i.e., uses) of ethical terms and the function of reasoning in ethics, we will see that the very function of ethical reasoning is to harmonize desires. But Hare suggests that his proponent of manhood might remain completely unimpressed by such talk about usage and doggedly insist, "It seems to me that the development of manhood is a cause superior to all others, and provides the only good reason for any moral conclusion."

Hare continues, ". . . it would be clear that what was dividing us was a moral difference. To say that all we were differing about was the meaning of the word 'ethics' would be unplausible."[13]

Here is an example to clarify what Hare means by "a moral difference." If two people disagree over whether vitamin C helps prevent colds, they could eventually settle this *factual* disagreement by investigating the facts—by taking the vitamin themselves and observing the results, by making statistical studies of its effects on others, and so on.

But ethical disagreements (or "moral differences") don't work that way. A pro-abortionist and an anti-abortionist could investigate the abortion issue until they both learned all there is to know about the subject. But this would not guarantee that both of them would end up favoring abortions, or that both would come out against abortion.

Similarly, two parties could agree on the facts about hunting, gambling, or promoting nuclear power, and still disagree over whether these practices are good or bad. They could see eye to eye on all the facts surrounding any issue and still be divided by a "moral difference."

Toulmin (Continued): Challenges From Hare

Getting back to Hare's criticism of Toulmin, Hare is pointing out that no amount of observation and agreement about the anthropological data and other relevant facts would necessarily lead to moral agreement between a Toulminian and Hare's proponent of manhood. Rather, the proponent of manhood is making a moral assertion when he says that the development of manhood provides the only good reason for any moral conclusion. Similarly, Toulmin is making a moral assertion when he says that "This practice would involve the least conflict of interests" is a *good* reason for "This would be the right practice."

What all this indicates, according to Hare, is that when Toulmin passes from a factual premise (such as "This practice would involve the least conflict of interest") to a moral one (e.g., "This would be the right practice,") and claims that the inference is justified by the logical criterion appropriate to ethics, there *is* a *moral* premise for this deduction after all. The logical criterion for ethics itself serves as the necessary moral premise. In his review, Hare makes this point as follows:

> Thus we might represent his view of moral reasoning by means of the following schema: $\frac{F}{E}$ where F is a conjunction of statements of 'ethically neutral' fact, and E is a moral conclusion. If this is to be a valid inference, there must be a rule of inference (say R) to the effect that inferences of this form are valid. (R might be '"This practice would involve the least conflict of interest attainable under the circumstances" is a good reason for "This would be the right practice"'.) Now I have given reasons for holding that R expresses a moral judgment. But if it does, then it is in the nature of a general moral rule, and the inference consists in nothing more novel than the subsumption of a particular set of circumstances under this rule.[14]

64   Toulmin (Continued): Challenges From Hare

Hare is telling us that Toulmin's rule of inference (what Toulmin calls the logical criterion for ethics) really amounts to a moral principle which can serve as a major premise of a syllogism.

Hare continues:

> We have, in fact, nothing more startling than a recognizable variant of the familiar Aristotelian practical syllogism: R
> $$\frac{F}{E}$$
> where R is a general moral rule, F a statement of fact subsuming some particular circumstances under the rule, and E a particular moral conclusion.[15]

And of course such an inference conforms to the rules of ordinary deduction.

The great danger of Toulmin's tactic, according to Hare, is that Toulmin might convince us that he can do something which logic cannot do:

> By dressing up the inference in this way, he suggests to the reader that, what logic cannot do, Mr. Toulmin can, namely infer a moral conclusion without having a moral premiss. The trick is performed only by smuggling in the essential moral premiss disguised as a rule of inference.[16]

Hare's conclusion is that Toulmin's attempt to derive moral judgments from facts has failed, just as the less sophisticated attempts to base moral justification on facts failed at the hands of our other philosophers—Aristotle, Mill, Moore, and Prichard. Assuming Hare is right, this means that there is an essential flaw in Toulmin's account of the way moral judgments are derived—and justified. It will follow, then, that Toulmin has failed to account for ultimate justification.

CRITERIA TO CLARIFY THE IDEA OF ULTIMATE JUSTIFICATION

Thanks to Hare's critique of Toulmin, our notion of ultimate justification, or proof of moral obligation, can be clarified further. As Hare has shown, even if Toulmin is correct in saying that reasons in terms of harmonizing desires are inevitably used in all communities, we can still intelligently question *whether* we ought to prescribe the use of reasons of that type, and *why* such reasons are good reasons.

A justification which can be questioned in such a way is not ultimate because, by ultimate justification, we mean a reason or set of reasons for doing an act which is complete in the sense of being self-sufficient and independent of further reasons. But if one can challenge the justification with questions which it has not thoroughly answered, further reasons will have to be provided. The justification will not be independent of further reasons, and it will not be self-sufficient as a proof.

For a justification to be ultimate, then, it must satisfy another criterion: there must be no room in it for any further questioning. If one can still ask meaningfully, "Should I favor reasons in terms of harmonizing desires?" or, "Why should I favor reasons in terms of harmonizing desires?" or any other meaningful questions that challenge the justification, the justification is dependent on further reasons, and therefore is incomplete.

This is the last of four tests or criteria we have articulated to help clarify the concept of ultimate justification. To restate them briefly, from Moore we learned that justification must not rely on the premise that pleasure or any other natural or metaphysical quality or thing is goodness per se (the naturalistic fallacy).

Secondly, thanks to Prichard, it became evident that the justification must not merely establish the goodness of the *goal* of the act. The justification must show that *obligation* pertains to the *act* itself.

The third criterion was derived from Ayer: The justification must include a guarantee of the truth or certainty of any idea or principle it depends on. It will be less than ultimate if, for example, one of its links is a contestable intuition (e.g., that lying is wrong), or is a declaration of mere faith (e.g., that one ought to do God's will).

Fourth, Toulmin and Hare have led us to the insight that a justification is less than ultimate if one can challenge it with questions it does not thoroughly answer.

Although there might be additional criteria or other ways to make the concept of ultimate justification more complete and precise, we seem to have arrived at a usable conception. It may help to formulate a concise description of what we are looking for during the rest of our study; and the following description should suffice as a tentative working formulation. Also, the four criteria above are related to the parts of the formulation as indicated: Our ultimate justification, or proof of moral obligation, must be a reason, set of reasons, or demonstration which is clear and rational (first criterion), which tells why one ought to do an act (second criterion), which allows no doubt about its truth or validity (third criterion), and which precludes any further questions as to whether or why one ought to do the act (fourth criterion).

A DILEMMA: ARBITRARY PREMISES OR NON-MORAL ONES

When Toulmin tried to derive moral judgments from facts, he was following in the footsteps of our other moralists. We have surveyed several philosophers who claimed to provide a basis for moral obligation. All of them, like Toulmin, used as the basis for moral obligation something they believed was *factual*. Mill based obligation on facts about pleasure; Aristotle used facts about well-being; and other naturalists, whom we mentioned briefly, relied on facts about other phenomena within nature such as evolution or satisfaction of interests.

Metaphysical ethical theorists such as Spinoza and the Thomists, based justification on what they believed were facts about something outside of nature, for example, God or realizing one's *true* self.

Intuitionists of Moore's type claimed to base justification on facts that one intuits about goodness, while intuitionists in Prichard's camp relied on intuited facts about the rightness or oughtness of the act itself.[20]

Why have so many philosophers considered facts—empirical, metaphysical, or intuited—to be the proper foundation for an ethical system? After Hume's warning about the impossibility of deducing obligation from fact, one would think that they would not be so persistent in committing this mistake.

Hare answers by pointing out the appealing nature of a theory grounded in fact: such a theory can claim to produce positive answers to difficult or controversial moral questions. Naturalistic, metaphysical, and intuitionist ethical theories, which together Hare calls "descriptivism"

> treat moral judgements as statements of fact. . . . Their purpose is to enable us to say to those who are in moral perplexity, and also to those who doubt or reject the standard moral rules, that these rules have a status like, for example, the fact that ice is lighter than water.[17]

As Hare makes these comments, he has Toulmin in mind along with the other descriptivists. In fact, he called Toulmin's theory "nothing but a highly sophisticated form of naturalism."[18] In another place, when discussing naturalism, Hare further explains the apparent advantage of being able to deduce how one ought to act from factual propositions:

> The method of naturalism is so to characterize the *meanings* of the key moral terms that, given certain factual premises, not themselves moral judgements, moral conclusions can be deduced from them. If this could be done, it was thought that it would be of great assistance to us in making moral decisions; we should only have to find out the non-moral facts, and the moral conclusion as to what we ought to do would follow. Those who say that it cannot be done leave themselves the task of giving an alternative account of moral reasoning.[19]

We can follow the implications of this passage and explain more fully why moral justification evidently must ultimately be grounded in fact: Making moral decisions is a process of reasoning out conclusions about how to act. But such reasoning requires premises to reason from. If the premises are not factual, they cannot be verified, and therefore must be considered arbitrary. And the conclusions deduced from them will not be justified. That is to say, if an ethical system is not grounded in facts (empirical, metaphysical, intuited, or any other kind), it must be a matter of feeling or attitude, or in some way arbitrary.

As Hare said in the above passage, those who would like to avoid any form of descriptivism leave themselves the task of giving an alternative account of moral reasoning. Or we might say the reason why so many philosophers have considered facts to be the proper foundation for an ethical system is that there seems to be no other adequate foundation.

The only other way out seems to be to take a stand closer to that of Ayer—i.e., to resort to a theory which acknowledges that the premises of moral reasoning reflect nothing more substantial than feelings or attitudes. It would then follow that so-called moral conclusions, likewise, merely express feelings.

We seem to be in a dilemma. If there is to be a firm basis for our deliberations, we must endorse a theory which is ultimately grounded in fact. But our survey of a number of theories and Hare's criticisms of Toulmin have shown that although a factual foundation may have a certain firmness, moral conclusions cannot be derived from it.[20] The other horn of the dilemma is to face this demoralizing truth and, with the emotivists, give up our hope that moral judgments can be justified—and therewith our hope of finding an account of ultimate justification.

NOTES

[1] Hare, "Review," *The Philosophical Quarterly*, 1 (1951), 373.

[2] Cf. O. A. Johnson, *Moral Knowledge* (The Hague: Martinus Nijhoff, 1966), p. 82: "For Toulmin the fact that the end of social

harmony justifies our moral judgments has nothing to do with the intrinsic goodness of social harmony but rests simply on the contingent fact, which he has observed, that people *do* accept the appeal to social harmony as a good reason for moral action, and act accordingly. Thus, Toulmin holds that the final justification for the view that a good reason is one that promotes social harmony is that it is the reason which people do as a matter of fact accept."

[3] Toulmin, *The Place of Reason in Ethics*, p. 101.
[4] *Ibid.*, p. 136.
[5] *Ibid.*, p. 133.
[6] *Ibid.*, p. 136.
[7] *Ibid.*, p. 223.
[8] David Hume, *A Treatise of Human Nature*, Book III, Part I, Sect. I.
[9] In another book, *The Uses of Argument*, Toulmin gives a much more thorough defense of his thesis that modes of logic vary from one context to another. He argues that only in a field like mathematics are we limited to strict deductive or "analytic" argument. A looser inference, "substantial" argument, is proper for most fields including ethics:

> "If we are going to hold out for analyticity, therefore, we shall find a general problem arising over all fields of argument other than analytic ones. Claims to knowledge, however well-founded they may appear in practice, are never going to come up to the philosopher's ideal standard. Once we have accepted this ideal, there seems no hope of salvaging our everyday claims to knowledge—pure mathematics apart. . . ." *The Uses of Argument* (Cambridge: Cambridge University Press, 1958), p. 223.
>
> "Our key distinction has been the distinction between *analytic* and *substantial* arguments; and this distinction has to be made, and insisted on, before the habitual ambiguities underlying most epistemological debates can be disentangled.
>
> "The only real way out of these epistemological difficulties is (I say) giving up the analytic ideal. Analytic criteria, whether of conclusiveness, demonstrativeness, necessity, certainty, validity, or justification, are beside the point when we are dealing with substantial arguments." *The Uses of Argument*, p. 234.

[10] R. M. Hare, "Review of *An Examination of the Place of Reason in Ethics*," *The Philosophical Quarterly*, 1 (1951), 372. Also see *The Language of Morals*, pp. 45–46.

[11] Hare, "Review," p. 373.

[12] *Ibid.*, p. 374.

[13] *Ibid.*

[14] *Ibid.*

[15] *Ibid.*

[16] *Ibid.*

[17] R. M. Hare, "The Practical Relevance of Philosophy," in his *Essays on Philosophical Method* (Los Angeles: University of California Press, 1972), p. 111.

[18] See Hare's article, "Broad's Approach to Moral Philosophy," in *Essays on Philosophical Method*, p. 15.

[19] R. M. Hare, *Freedom and Reason* (Oxford: Oxford University Press, 1963), p. 86.

[20] This reference to ethical theories having factual bases may remind us of the often made claim that teleological theories are ultimately based on non-moral values while deontological theories are not. Cf. Frankena's comment about moral philosophers: "In general their views have been of two sorts: (1) *deontological* theories and (2) *teleological* ones. A teleological theory says that the basic or ultimate criterion or standard of what is morally right, wrong, obligatory, etc., is the nonmoral value that is brought into being." (*Ethics*, p. 13). However, let us not forget that the conclusion we have reached is much more sweeping. Our analysis has shown that not only teleological theories, but also deontological ones like those of Prichard and Ross, are ultimately based on something factual and non-moral. As Hare puts it, "if the word 'good' is treated in the fashion that many intuitionists have treated it . . . sentences containing the word as so understood will not be genuine evaluative judgements, because no imperatives can be derived from them. But this objection applies, not only to the intuitionist theory of 'good', but to all who insist on the solely factual character of moral judgements; it applies to Prichard himself." (*The Language of Morals*, p. 30).

Part Two

Hare's Analysis of Moral Justification

Part Two

Kant's Analysis of Moral Justification

V

Hare's *The Language of Morals:* How We Deduce Moral Principles

THERE CAN BE VALID DEDUCTION FROM PRESCRIPTIVE PREMISES

From the concluding section of the last chapter, it seems that in order to have ultimate justification, we must find premises which are neither factual nor arbitrary. For, as Hare argued against Toulmin, from factual premises only factual conclusions can be deduced, not moral conclusions. But if we start with non-factual, arbitrary premises, our conclusions will be arbitrary.

Even if we could find premises for ethical reasoning which were non-factual without being arbitrary, it would seem that valid deductions could not proceed from them. It has been generally assumed by logicians that logical deductions can contain only factual or indicative sentences. Hare points this out in the opening sentence of the first article he published:

> It has often been taken for granted by logicians that there is a class of sentences which is the proper subject-matter of logic, and that they are at liberty to ignore all sentences which are not included in this class. . . . The sort of sentences which are to be admitted into the logical fold are variously referred to as 'scientific', 'cognitive', 'informative', 'fact-stating', 'true-or-false', 'theoretical', 'referential', 'symbolic', etc; and the sort

of sentences which are to be excluded are called 'emotive', 'evocative', 'non-fact-stating', etc. The latter are held not to state genuine propositions, and therefore, since propositions are the bricks out of which a logical system is built, to be altogether beyond the pale of such a system.[1]

If logically valid reasoning cannot be built out of non-fact-stating sentences, there will not be much point in our looking for reliable non-fact-stating premises. Therefore, before trying again to find a kind of non-fact-stating and unarbitrary premise for ethical reasoning, we had better show that reasoning involving such sentences can be logically valid.

In the article just quoted, Hare proceeds to argue that logical deductions *can* contain non-fact-stating sentences. He outlines the article as follows.

> I shall take a class of sentences, namely imperatives, which clearly do not purport to state that anything is the case, and shall show that their logical behaviour is in many respects as exemplary as that of indicative sentences, and in particular that it is possible to infer an imperative conclusion from imperative premisses.[2]

We can pass over much of Hare's analysis, which he gives in detail in this article and elsewhere;[3] and we can quickly make his case plausible by first letting him point out the logical behavior of imperatives (or "commands") with regard to contradiction:

> Commands as well as statements can contradict one another. Even if this were not a normal way of speaking, we might well adopt it; for the feature to which it draws attention in commands is identical with that which is normally called contradiction. Consider the following example, taken from Lord

Cunningham's autobiography. The admiral and the captain of a cruiser which is his flagship shout almost simultaneously to the helmsman in order to avoid a collision, one 'Hard 'a port' and the other 'Hard 'a starboard'. Lord Cunningham refers to these two orders as 'contrary'; and so they are, in the proper Aristotelian sense. It follows that the two orders contradict one another in the sense that the conjunction of them is self-contradictory; the relation between them is the same as that between the two predictions 'You are going to turn hard 'a port' and 'You are going to turn hard 'a starboard'. Some orders can, of course, be contradictory without being contrary; the simple contradictory of 'Shut the door' is 'Do not shut the door'.[4]

It is clear that imperatives can contradict one another. But Hare still must show that *deductions* can occur among imperatives. He begins by pointing out that the function of logical words like "all" is such that "to know the meaning of the word 'all' is to know that one cannot without self-contradiction say certain things, for example "All men are mortal and Socrates is a man but Socrates is not mortal."[5]

He explains that the role of these words in commands is such that there must be entailment relations among commands:

> Now the word 'all' and other logical words are used in commands, as in statements. It follows that there must also be entailment-relations between commands; for otherwise it would be impossible to give any meaning to these words as used in them.[6]

He illustrates with an example: Because of the meaning of the word "all," the command "Take all the boxes to the station" logically entails the command "Take this to the station"—if this is one of the boxes:

> If we had to find out whether someone knew the meaning of the word 'all' in 'Take all the boxes to the station', we should have to find out whether he realized that a person who assented to this command, and also to the statement 'This is one of the boxes' and yet refused to assent to the command 'Take this to the station' could only do so if he had misunderstood one of these three sentences.[7]

He concludes that "the existence in our language of universal sentences in the imperative mood is in itself sufficient proof that our language admits of entailments of which at least one term is a command."[8]

Although Hare spoke of non-moral commands such as "Take all the boxes to the station," he applies what he said about deductive validity to *moral* commands and to other kinds of moral utterances as well. A moral assertion may have the grammatical form of a command, e.g., "Love thy neighbor," or it may have the grammatical form of an indicative, e.g., "One ought to love his neighbor," or "It is right to do so and so." But despite the grammatical similarity of sentences containing "ought" and "right" to factual (indicative) propositions, the logical role of these moral assertions is more like that of commands and imperatives.

The reason for their similarity to commands is as follows. Both moral principles, e.g., "One ought to love his neighbor," and particular maxims, e.g., "I ought to help Smith," have a great deal to do with guiding behavior and expressing decisions about how to act. They do not merely describe facts. In one way or another, such utterances guide or point out how one is to act. It may be a moral principle commanding or recommending general modes of behavior (People ought to love their neighbors) or the particular conclusion of someone's deliberation about his own behavior (e.g., the maxim, "I ought to help Smith"). In either case such utterances do something which can be described as commanding, advising, commending, resolving, and so on.

To use Hare's more general term for this function, moral principles and particular maxims are all *prescriptive* utterances. In Hare's words, "The function of moral principles is to guide conduct. The language of morals is one sort of prescriptive language."[9]

Thus, although moral assertions may have different grammatical forms, they all have the logical function essential to commands, i.e., they are prescriptive. Therefore, the possibility of making valid deductions, which Hare showed to pertain to commands, will also pertain to moral assertions.[10] This point can be made still clearer with a brief example: Consider the moral principle "One ought not to lie." Even if this assertion is non-factual, it should now be clear that the following would be a logically valid deduction: "One ought not to lie. Telling Jones I was ill would be a lie. Therefore, I ought not to tell Jones I was ill."

In conclusion, it should now be clear that there can indeed be logically valid deductions containing non-fact-stating moral sentences.

PRESCRIPTIVE AND FACTUAL PREMISES ARE BOTH NEEDED

To find out whether Hare can account for ultimate justification, we must next see how he analyzes the overall structure of moral reasoning. Although the foregoing section has shown how moral reasoning can be strict deduction from non-fact-stating premises, we must also analyze the overall structure of moral reasoning. It is necessary to understand this structure before we can tackle the more difficult question of whether Hare accounts for moral premises which are both non-fact-stating and unarbitrary.

In our example of moral reasoning, in addition to the prescriptive major premise ("One ought not to lie") and the prescriptive conclusion ("I ought not to tell Jones I was ill"), there was also a factual minor premise ("Telling Jones I was ill would be a lie"). With a little reflection, it can be seen that whenever a chain of moral reasoning culminates in a conclusion about doing a particular act, that reasoning must have included a premise which spelled out the *facts* of the situation. Hare explains as follows:

> We plainly cannot decide what to do unless we know at least something about what we should be doing if we did this or that. For example, suppose that I am an employer, and am wondering whether or not to sack a clerk who habitually turns up at the office after the hour at which he has undertaken to turn up. If I sack him I shall be depriving his family of the money on which they live, perhaps giving my firm a reputation which will lead clerks to avoid it when other jobs are available, and so on; if I keep him, I shall be causing the other clerks to do work which otherwise would be done by this clerk; and the affairs of the office will not be transacted so quickly as they would if all the clerks were punctual. These would be the sorts of considerations that I should take into account in making my decision.[11]

It is clear that before one can responsibly reach a decision, he must have in mind at least one factual proposition indicating the facts of the case. As will become more clear below, this serves as one of the premises in the agent's reasoning.

It remains true that the more general *prescriptive* premise is essential as well. To show why this is so, I would like to expand upon Hare's example.

Suppose I understand the effects of firing the clerk: harm to his family, fewer people applying for jobs with my company, but greater efficiency within the office, and so on. This knowledge alone does not produce the decision "I would fire the clerk" or "I will keep him." I must favor a principle or policy which will give me a way to interpret or make use of these facts. For example, I must tend to favor punctuality over the other considerations; or I must believe that kindness should come before business efficiency. In other words, before I can frame a decision out of the facts about the clerk, I must have in mind a more general principle, e.g., "One ought to get rid of tardy employees regardless of harm to their families" or "One ought at all costs to avoid the dangers of tardiness spreading among employees" or "It is wrong to put business interests ahead of humanitarian concerns."

Although any example like this greatly oversimplifies the reasoning process, by now it should be clear that mere factual information is not enough to produce a decision as to how one ought to act. To reach a decision the agent must have certain policies or attitudes,[12] i.e., prescriptive principles, enabling him to assign priority to the various factual considerations. Since these prescriptive principles are more general, they take the role of major premises in moral reasoning, with the more specific factual propositions serving as the minor premises.

In short, inspection of the logical elements essential to the process of making moral decisions reveals that there must be (1) a major premise consisting of a prescriptive moral principle, (2) a factual minor premise which identifies the particular act as being of the type referred to by the major premise, and (3) the prescriptive conclusion which asserts that the particular act should be done.

Incidentally, the foregoing analysis also serves as a way of defending Hume's thesis, which was mentioned earlier, "No 'ought' from an 'is'." Hare elucidates that thesis as follows:

> It is now generally regarded as true by definition that (to speak roughly at first) nothing can appear in the conclusion of a valid deductive inference which is not, from their very meaning, implicit in the conjunction of the premises. It follows that, if there is an imperative in the conclusion, not only must *some* imperative appear in the premises, but that very imperative must be itself implicit in them.[13]

To guard against future misunderstanding, it should be noted that some sentences appear to be factual while actually being evaluative. Suppose that in the foregoing quote, instead of saying, "If I sack him I shall be depriving his family of the money on which they live," the employer had said, "I shall be depriving his family of money which they *deserve*." His statement would not have been purely factual. Because of its use of the word "deserve," it would contain an implicit moral judgment. In effect, the employer would be saying, "I shall be depriving his family of money which they *ought* to receive."

Or consider this syllogism, which at first may seem to conform to the pattern we have outlined: "One ought to keep promises. By paying Smith five dollars, I would be keeping a promise. Therefore, I ought to pay him." At first glance, the minor premise might seem to be purely factual. But it can be argued that usually by using the word "promise" one indicates that he assents to the institution of promising, and thus is implicitly making a moral assertion.[14] Therefore such sentences are not purely factual and, thus, are not the sort we have in mind when we speak of factual minor premises.

Accordingly, when we speak of facts or of "factual minor premises," we are referring to statements which are simply objective descriptions, not to those which are implicitly prescriptive or evaluative.[15]

UNLIKE DESCRIPTIVISM, PRESCRIPTIVISM ALLOWS FOR MORAL *DECISION*

Although the logical structure of moral reasoning has now been mapped out, we are still faced with our earlier and more difficult puzzle. In avoiding the mistake of relying on factual premises alone, doesn't Hare get caught on the other horn of the dilemma? Since the major premises of moral reasoning such as "One ought to love his neighbor," are prescriptive and non-fact-stating, aren't they inevitably arbitrary? Can Hare somehow show that they are objectively based, or that one's choice of such principles is not arbitrary?

According to Hare, if one understands how we decide on moral principles, it will become clear that those decisions are not arbitrary at all. Hare calls such choices "decisions of principle." The first step in understanding how we decide on moral principles is to see that such decisions are moral rather than intellectual. To clarify this distinction, it will help first to show how descriptivist theories have failed to explain—or even acknowledge—the factor of decision. Speaking of the descriptivists' neglect, Hare says:

> The gravest error, however, of the type of theory which I am criticizing is that it leaves out of our reasoning about conduct a factor which is of the very essence of morals. This factor is decision.[16]

Although Hare does not explicitly say so in *The Language of Morals*, from our own analysis in the preceding chapters, we can see that every descriptivist theory inevitably depicts decision-making as a rigid intellectual process and does not make clear how there can be any room for individual free choice or moral weakness. Since the moralists we considered before turning to Hare construed the major premise in moral deliberation as factual (e.g., "Pleasure is good," or "It is wrong to lie"), these descriptivists did not depict such a major premise as something the agent makes a moral choice about. Rather, the agent merely observes or perceives the empirical fact that pleasure is desirable and good; or he somehow witnesses the intuited *fact* that lying is wrong, and so on. Thus, the descriptivist theory fails to explain how accepting or rejecting such principles is any more than a process of perception, intuition, or intellect.

The minor premise (e.g., "Telling Jones I was ill would be a lie") likewise is a matter of fact to be recognized as true or false, and not something requiring a responsible moral decision. Finally, since the conclusion is logically inferred from the premises, there certainly is no leeway in that analytic process of entailment for anything we could call responsible decision-making.

Thus, the descriptivists portray moral decision-making purely as an intellectual process, and they give no insight as to how the agent can go wrong in his moral thinking, as long as he perceives or intuits accurately and reasons logically.

It may seem as if we are claiming that error is impossible according to descriptivists, but we are not. Rather, we are suggesting that since descriptivism depicts immoral decision-making as nothing but error in perception, intuition, or reasoning, descriptivism cannot be a satisfactory theory. Being mistaken in one's moral thinking surely must involve more than mere inefficiency or malfunctioning of our perceptive or reasoning faculties.

In other words, the implications of descriptivism are that *if* the agent properly carries out the process outlined by descriptivists, he cannot go wrong. Of course, that "if" is significant: The agent won't always carry out the process properly; he will often misperceive, misintuit, or reason invalidly, and thus err. But it should be clear that according to descriptivism, failure to reach the right decision must be due merely to that sort of error, i.e., to malfunctioning of our perceptive, intuitive, or reasoning faculties, and not to anything we could call immoral *decision*.

However, moral life is not so simple; and Hare, like the existentialists, alerts us to the fact that there must be something wrong with theories which depict moral deliberation as such an intellectual process.

Hare does not go so far as existentialists like Sartre in putting all of the burden of responsibility on the agent. As Hare points out, it is inevitable and proper for parents and teachers to play a major role in shaping a child's moral principles. The wise parent will also see to it that his child gradually develops the ability to decide about moral principles on his own. The parent must build in the child a solid foundation of moral principles and the ability and desire to change and improve these principles when necessary. This latter ability will require feelings of self-confidence and responsibility which the parent can instill in the child by giving him enough opportunity to make decisions on his own when he is young. In speaking about how the child learns from the parent to make decisions of principle, Hare says:

> It is very like learning to drive. It would be foolish, in teaching someone to drive, to try to inculcate into him such fixed and comprehensive principles that he would never have to make an independent decision. It would be equally foolish to go to the other extreme and leave it to him to find his own way of driving. What we do, if we are sensible, is to give him a solid basis of principles, but at the same time ample opportunity of making the decisions upon which these principles are based, and by which they are modified, improved, adapted to changed circumstances, or even abandoned if they become entirely unsuited to a new environment. To teach only the principles, without giving the opportunity of subjecting them to the learner's own decisions of principle, is like teaching science exclusively from textbooks without entering a laboratory. On the other hand, to abandon one's child or one's driving-pupil to his own self-expression is like putting a boy into a laboratory and saying 'Get on with it'. The boy may enjoy himself or kill himself, but will probably not learn much science.[17]

From this passage together with the rest of this section, it should now be clear that we must acknowledge a factor of decision which is central to ethics but disregarded by most theories. The next section will begin to clarify how, when making a decision about principles, one carries on that elusive process of moral *decision* per se.

DECISIONS OF PRINCIPLE MAY BE JUSTIFIED THANKS TO DEDUCTION AND FACTS

As we consider how one makes decisions of principle, this clarification should show how our choices of principles are not arbitrary.

Suppose I am new in my position as office manager, and am suddenly faced with the decision mentioned earlier about whether to fire the tardy clerk. Suppose further that I entered my job as office manager with a definite conviction that, in order to maintain efficiency, it is the duty of any office manager to fire tardy clerks.

The clerk in question, however, impresses me by describing hardships which would result from his losing his job. He also explains why he has been arriving late; and after a while it becomes apparent that there are promising ways to resolve his problem, e.g., by having him join a car pool. I decide that it is better to give him another chance instead of firing him.

Because of this experience, my outlook has now changed somewhat: I have decided that in a case like this it is better not to fire the employee right away, but to listen to his side and to try to find other ways to remedy his tardiness. Thus, my earlier conviction or principle, "Always fire tardy clerks," has now changed into "Fire tardy clerks only if there are no kinder ways to cure their tardiness."

How was this decision of principle made? One essential ingredient in the making of it was consideration of the *facts* of the case, viz., facts about what would happen if I fired the clerk, facts regarding the car pool, and so on. Another ingredient was certain *other principles* of mine which enabled me to interpret and evaluate the facts— e.g., "Be sympathetic to those in trouble," "One ought to treat others as he himself would like to be treated," and so on.

One small segment of my reasoning may have been the syllogism: "One ought to be sympathetic to those in trouble. This clerk is in trouble. Therefore, I ought to be sympathetic to him." In arriving at the particular conclusion to give the clerk another chance, I have also decided on a new principle, viz., that one ought not to fire employees unless there are no kinder ways to resolve their tardiness.

Notice that the elements involved in deciding on this new principle were the same as those we found necessary for reaching any *particular* moral conclusion: (1) prescriptive principles serving as major premises, (2) factual minor premises, and (3) deductive inference.

Although the major premises (i.e., an agent's other principles such as "Be sympathetic to those in trouble") may be arbitrary as far as we know at this time, the other two ingredients—the factual minor premises and the deductive pattern of inference—are anything but arbitrary. Thus, we have made some progress toward showing that decisions of principle are not arbitrary, and therefore can have the kind of justification we have been seeking.

NOTES

[1] R. M. Hare, "Imperative Sentences," *Mind*, 58 (1949), p. 39. Reprinted in R. M. Hare, *Practical Inferences* (Los Angeles: University of California Press, 1972), p. 1.

[2] Hare, "Imperative Sentences" in *Practical Inferences*, p. 2.

[3] See the following articles by Hare in *Practical Inferences*: "Some Alleged Differences between Imperatives and Indicatives," "Practical Inferences," "Meaning and Speech Acts," and Chapter 2 of *The Language of Morals*.

⁴ Hare, *The Language of Morals*, p. 22.
⁵ *Ibid.*, p. 24.
⁶ *Ibid.*, p. 25.
⁷ *Ibid.*
⁸ *Ibid.*, p. 26.
⁹ *Ibid.*, p. 1. Cf. also p. 2 ff., and *Freedom and Reason*, p. 4.
¹⁰ *The Language of Morals*, p. 55.
¹¹ *Ibid.*, p. 56.
¹² For Hare's use of the term "attitude" see *Ibid.*, p. 70.
¹³ *Ibid.*, p. 32. Also see p. 29. This line of reasoning can of course be developed into a refutation of naturalism and other descriptive theories. See *Ibid.*, p. 30.
¹⁴ Cf. R. M. Hare, "The Promising Game," *Revue Internationale de Philosophe*, 70 (1964), pp. 398–412. Reprinted in W. D. Hudson, ed., *The Is-Ought Question* (London: Macmillan and Co., Ltd., 1969), pp. 144–156.
¹⁵ Another distinction we should make is between consequences of acts and types of acts. In the above quotation, to illustrate what he meant by a fact, Hare gave as examples various effects or consequences of the proposed act, e.g., depriving the clerk's family of money. On the other hand, earlier on the same page, when outlining the two kinds of premises in moral reasoning, Hare used as an example of a factual minor premise a description of an act as falling under a certain type, viz., speaking falsely:

> The major premiss is a principle of conduct; the minor premiss is a statement, more or less full, of what we should in fact be doing if we did one or other of the alternatives open to us. Thus if I decide not to say something, because it is false, I am acting on a principle, 'Never (or never under certain conditions) say what is false', and I must know that this, which I am wondering whether to say, is false. (*The Language of Morals*, p. 56)

Hare is indicating that the syllogism involved here would be something like: "Never say what is false. This which I am thinking of saying is false. Therefore, I ought not to say it." The factual minor premise merely identifies the proposed act as being a certain type, without focusing attention on its consequences.

Despite this distinction, both consequences and types of acts can be purely matters of fact. To state that a clerk's family will be deprived of money is not, under normal circumstances, to make a value judgment, not even implicitly. Nor are we uttering an indirect moral judgment when we assert that a proposed statement would be false.

It seems perfectly legitimate for Hare to use the word "fact" to refer to both things: consequences and types of acts.

[16] *Ibid.*, p. 54.
[17] *Ibid.*, p. 76.

VI

Hare's *The Language of Morals* (Continued): Are Our Moral Decisions Fully Justified?

DOES ATTENTION TO FACTS KEEP PRINCIPLES FROM BEING ARBITRARY?

The foregoing chapter has shown that the process of deciding about principles is just as logical as the process of deciding about one's particular moral acts. On second thought, we will now see that there still seems to be an arbitrary, i.e., unjustified, element in those decisions of principle.

In reasoning about whether to adopt or change a principle, we use as major premises other principles which we already hold—which I will call "prior principles."[1] So far, it has not been demonstrated how there can be justification for these prior principles. Thus, prior principles would seem to be at least somewhat arbitrary. Therefore, our decisions of principle, which depend on those prior principles, would seem to be somewhat arbitrary also.

Hare would defend himself against this new charge by asking us to take a fresh look at the role of facts. To the extent that the agent is thoughtful and careful, he is continually testing and adjusting his principles by observing and analyzing whatever facts are relevant to the problem at hand. It seems that theoretically one could make decisions of principle exclusively by analyzing facts about the effects of his acts.

Hare asks us to imagine a clairvoyant who would have total knowledge of the effects of all the courses of action open to him. At each moment, he could make a fresh assessment of his situation; and his complete godlike foresight would enable him to see instantly which course of action would produce the set of effects he preferred. Therefore, he would not have to rely on established guidelines for acting, that is, on prior principles.

> Let us suppose that a man has a peculiar kind of clairvoyance such that he can know everything about the effects of all the alternative actions open to him. But let us suppose that he has so far formed for himself, or been taught, no principles of conduct. In deciding between alternative courses of action, such a man would know, fully and exactly, between what he was deciding. We have to ask to what extent, if any, such a man would be handicapped, in coming to a decision, by not having any formed principles. It would seem beyond doubt that he could choose between two courses; it would be strange, even, to call such a choice necessarily arbitrary or ungrounded; for if a man knows to the last detail exactly what he is doing, and what he might otherwise have done, his choice is not arbitrary in the sense in which a choice would be arbitrary if made by the toss of a coin without any consideration of the effects.[2]

The clairvoyant's knowledge of the facts would enable him to foresee which kinds of acts would achieve what he wanted. On this basis, he could choose which types of acts to perform. But in choosing which types of acts to perform, he in effect would be deciding what principles to have. For to commit oneself to a certain type of act is to have a principle of behavior. Thus, he would be making decisions of principle on the basis of facts without relying on any prior principles. (Of course, his desires and inclinations would cause him to prefer one set of effects over another. More will be said about this in the next two chapters.)

Hare expresses these insights as follows:

> Although we have assumed that the man has no formed principles, he shows . . . that he has started to form principles for himself; for to choose effects *because* they are such and such is to begin to act on a principle that such and such effects are to be chosen. We see in this example that in order to act on principle it is not necessary in some sense to have a principle already, before you act; it may be that the decision to act in a certain way, because of something about the effects of acting in that way, *is* to subscribe to a principle of action.[3]

Because the rest of us cannot foresee what all the effects of the various courses of action would be, we ordinary people cannot make decisions by paying attention to the effects alone. We depend on guidelines or established policies as well, i.e., on prior principles. Thus, in real life, we must always use prior principles as major premises when making decisions of principle.

Insofar as we are wise and responsible, we keep testing those prior principles by appealing to the facts. The mature and wise individual is continually validating, adjusting, or re-establishing his principles on the basis of facts; and his principles thereby become less and less arbitrary.

Less independent individuals will tend to coast along on the principles they were taught, without being critical or trying to improve them on the basis of experience with the facts. As Hare puts it, individuals of this sort "act on the principles without thinking, and their power of making considered decisions of principle becomes atrophied. They act always by the book."[4] Their principles are less tested and less fully justified—or more arbitrary. Accordingly, it seems the more thoughtful and responsible one is (the more he approaches the ideal of the clairvoyant), the more his principles are based on the facts—and the less arbitrary they are.

HAS HARE EXPLAINED AWAY THE FACTOR OF DECISION?

In emphasizing how principles can be very thoroughly grounded in factual experience, Hare may seem to be regressing to descriptivism and explaining away the factor of decision. He may seem to be saying that principles are justified insofar as they are derived from facts. According to our earlier analysis, if principles were derived from facts, they would be strictly deduced from—and thus rigidly determined by—those facts. As we saw, this would be an intellectual and objective process, lacking in the factor of responsible *decision-making*.

On the contrary, Hare would insist that even if an agent could base a decision of principle solely on factual considerations, the element of choice would still come into play. For example, if the clairvoyant makes a decision by considering only the effects, and without being guided by any principles, he still has to *choose* which effects he prefers. In the following passage the clairvoyant expresses this ability to choose:

But suppose that we were to ask such a man 'Why did you choose this set of effects rather than that? Which of the many effects were they that led you to decide the way you did?' His answer to this question might be of two kinds. He might say 'I can't give any reasons; I just felt like deciding that way; another time, faced with the same choice, I might decide differently'. On the other hand, he might say 'It was this and this that made me decide; I was deliberately avoiding such and such effects, and seeking such and such'. If he gave the first of these two answers, we might in a certain sense of that word call his decision arbitrary (though even in that case he had *some* reason for his choice, namely, that he felt that way); but if he gave the second, we should not.[5]

Thus, if the clairvoyant were making a decision solely by considering the effects of his acts, it would be entirely up to him to select which of these future states of affairs he preferred. His deciding in favor of one state rather than another would not be merely an intellectual process of perception, intuition, and deduction. Rather, he would be making a genuine decision to go after one set of effects rather than the other. Tomorrow, he might feel different and choose differently even though he was considering identical facts. Or, another clairvoyant in the same situation might decide differently too.

Accordingly, although in an ideal or theoretical situation an individual might make a decision of principle by considering effects alone, those facts do not logically dictate behavior in a way that precludes the agent's making his own decisions. Therefore, when Hare emphasizes how in ordinary life our principles can be thoroughly grounded in factual experience, he is not explaining away the factor of decision.

ARE DECISIONS JUSTIFIED THANKS TO LOGIC, PRINCIPLES, AND FACTS?

At this point, the following objection may arise: Despite what can be said about a clairvoyant, when it comes to ordinary people, all decisions of principle are based at least somewhat on the agent's prior principles. Since those prior principles are prescriptive and non-fact-stating, won't the resulting decisions of principle be at least somewhat arbitrary and lacking in justification? For example, although I may have analyzed the facts very carefully when making my decision to adopt the principle "Fire tardy clerks only when kinder methods fail," this decision still was partially due to my prior principle "Be sympathetic to those in trouble." Thus, this decision of principle was partially based on something non-factual and, therefore, must be at least partially arbitrary.

This objection can be answered by noting that my prior principle, "Be sympathetic to those in trouble," though non-fact-stating, was far from arbitrary. It, like the later principle, "Fire tardy clerks only when kinder methods fail," was the outcome of careful decisions of principle based on thoughtful observation and analysis of the anticipated effects.

If I had absorbed the principle "Be sympathetic to those in trouble" in Sunday school and in later life had never tested it on the basis of factual experiences, my holding of this principle could be called arbitrary. And later decisions of principle which depended on it, like the one about the firing of clerks, could also be called arbitrary; for they would be made "by the book." Nevertheless, the use of prior principles does not necessarily render a decision of principle arbitrary. If the agent is responsible and thoughtful, those prior principles will have been justified as well.

The essential point in all this is that for a principle to be justified or unarbitrary, it does not have to be deduced exclusively from factual propositions. We consider a principle to be justified as long as it is the result of deduction and decision on the basis of facts, plus other principles which have been carefully decided upon in the same way.

In a key passage in *The Language of Morals*, Hare explains how principles plus facts about effects work together to produce decisions that are fully justified. It will help to break this passage into four parts. First, regarding the question of the relative importance of principles and effects, Hare explains that you cannot say whether one or the other plays the greater part. Insofar as a decision is made on the basis of principles, it is in effect being made on the basis of consequences as well—since any principles which the decision relied on were chosen largely because of their consequences. And conversely, insofar as the decision is made on the basis of consequences, those consequences will largely be sought after because of principles which the agent holds (unless he is a principleless clairvoyant).

Hare says it this way:

> Sometimes, if asked why we did A, we say, 'Because it was a case falling under principle P', and if asked to justify P in turn, we go into the effects of observing it and of not observing it. But sometimes, when asked the same question 'Why did you do A? we say 'Because if I hadn't, E would have happened', and if asked what was wrong about E happening, we appeal to some principle.
>   The truth is that, if asked to justify as completely as possible any decision, we have to bring in both effects—to give content

to the decision—and principles, and the effects in general of observing those principles, and so on, until we have satisfied our inquirer.[6]

To completely spell out the justification of a decision would be an endless exercise:

> Thus a complete justification of a decision would consist of a complete account of its effects, together with a complete account of the principles which it observed, and the effects of observing those principles—for, of course, it is the effects (what obeying them in fact consists in) which give content to the principles too. Thus, if pressed to justify a decision completely, we have to give a complete specification of the way of life of which it is a part.[7]

Nevertheless, the agent must *decide* on those principles and consequences which make up that endless network of justification:

> If the inquirer still goes on asking 'But why *should* I live like that?' then there is no further answer to give him, because we have already, *ex hypothesi*, said everything that could be included in this further answer. We can only ask him to make up his own mind which way he ought to live; for in the end everything rests upon such a decision of principle. He has to decide whether to accept that way of life or not; if he accepts it, then we can proceed to justify the decisions that are based upon it; if he does not accept it, then let him accept some other, and try to live by it. The sting is in the last clause.[8]

Even so, such decisions are far from arbitrary:

> To describe such ultimate decisions as arbitrary, because *ex hypothesi* everything which could be used to justify them has

already been included in the decision, would be like saying that a complete description of the universe was utterly unfounded, because no further fact could be called upon in corroboration of it. This is not how we use the words 'arbitrary' and 'unfounded'. Far from being arbitrary, such a decision would be the most wellfounded of decisions, because it would be based upon a consideration of everything upon which it could possibly be founded.[9]

To summarize: for the responsible agent, a decision about principles is far from arbitrary, for it was reasoned out logically and with careful attention to the relevant facts. Also, the prior principles which contribute to the decision will also have been arrived at by the same careful and logical process. Finally, the agent's decisions about what specific acts to perform would seem to be fully justified as well—since they too are made on the basis of the justified principles just discussed, plus the relevant facts, and with strict deductive logic.

DEPENDENCE ON PRIOR PRINCIPLES WOULD KEEP A PRINCIPLE PARTLY UNCERTAIN

We have been working on the problem of how to account for moral judgments which are not essentially factual, but which are not arbitrary either. That is, we have been seeking an ethical system which accounts for the sort of firmness, objectivity, or unarbitrariness associated with descriptive theories by virtue of their factual bases. But we want an ethical system which at the same time is independent of factual bases. Now I am going to turn against Hare, and argue that despite the account of justification in *The Language of Morals* as just presented, Hare does not seem to have succeeded in developing such a system after all.

Let's suppose that a descriptivist such as Mill is right in saying that a good act is one which produces more pleasure than pain. Empirical investigation by sociologists may be able to establish with a high degree of certainty that more pleasure than pain is produced by certain acts (e.g., individuals in a high income bracket contributing to charities). Acts of this type will have been justified in some sense thanks to the factual nature of this process of justification. Or, if Prichard is correct in saying that we can *intuit* the fact that certain acts are right, we may be able to establish in a simpler way that giving to charity is right. Although for Prichard empirical investigation would not be necessary, the justification for the act would still have a high (or perhaps higher) degree of certainty or firmness because it would be based on clearcut knowledge of fact.

For Hare, justification of an act is not a purely factual matter. It is only partially based on factual considerations, and partially on one's prior principles. But according to the last section, since those prior principles are the result of very careful decisions of principle, we should not call them arbitrary.

Nevertheless, those principles are by no means as firmly or objectively justified as factual propositions can be. The flaw in Hare's argument seems to be the following: Although in the case of the clairvoyant a principle could theoretically be arrived at by considering nothing but facts, with ordinary people this does not happen. A person's new principles normally are deduced at least partly from previous principles he already held. But those prior principles were likewise deduced at least partly from still earlier principles (and partly from facts about effects). If the chain of principles were traced back and back, it would be found to extend through one's parents, ancestors, teachers, and the teachers' teachers, and so on. There would never be any one ultimate principle which was independent of such prior principles. There would be no ultimate principle which had a degree of firmness, objectivity, or certainty comparable to that of factual propositions.

The only rationale Hare seems to have for calling those principles "justified" is that they are chosen in a careful and thoughtful way on the basis of prior principles and facts about effects. What Hare has done is to *define* "justified" and "unarbitrary" so that to call a decision justified will mean that it has been carefully reasoned out. In other words, for Hare, "justified" or "unarbitrary" does not refer to a high degree of objective certainty; it has more to do with the degree of systematic effort the agent exerts when making his decisions of principle.

Hare's mistake is not that he has lapsed into descriptivism as the intuitionists and perhaps Toulmin did. He has erred in the other direction: his theory seems to be more like an extension of emotivism. Hare seems to be saying that as long as the agent has serious feelings about his decision-making and manifests a conscientious attitude by deliberating carefully, he cannot be accused of acting arbitrarily. Even if the agent were to make innocent errors in observing the facts or unintentional logical errors, one gets the impression that Hare would still hesitate to call the results unjustified. Hare's message in *The Language of Morals* seems to be that justification in ethics is primarily a function of the agent's attitude or the spirit of conscientiousness with which he carries on his decision-making.

In reacting to the foregoing objection, let us first note that it raises the whole question of what is meant by justification in ethics. Is it appropriate or meaningful to conceive of justification in ethics as involving the kind of objectivity that factual propositions can have? Perhaps the contemporary analysts are right in saying that the meaning of a term is its use in language, and perhaps Hare has accurately portrayed how we use the words "justification" and "arbitrary." If so, to say that a principle or act has ultimate justification will *mean* that it has been carefully reasoned out according to the procedure Hare has outlined. And to demand that ultimate justification involve a high degree of objectivity or certainty would be to misuse the term "ultimate justification."

If our study has to end on this note, it might seem like an anticlimax. We may feel disappointed in Hare for not living up to our expectations and demonstrating how justification in ethics can have a level of certainty or unarbitrariness comparable to that of factual propositions. Let us investigate Hare's second major book, *Freedom and Reason*, to see whether he can somehow satisfy the foregoing objection. Let's see whether *Freedom and Reason* demonstrates that moral principles can be fully justified so that they are as objective, certain, and unarbitrary as fully verified factual propositions are.

NOTES

[1] "Prior principles" is my term, not Hare's.
[2] *The Language of Morals*, p. 58.
[3] *Ibid.*, p. 59.
[4] *Ibid.*, p. 72.
[5] *Ibid.*, p. 58.

[6] *Ibid.*, p. 68.
[7] *Ibid.*, p. 69.
[8] *Ibid.*
[9] *Ibid.*

VII

Hare's *Freedom and Reason:* Justification as a Function of Logical Consistency

MORAL REASONING IS TESTING PRINCIPLES BY CHECKING CONSEQUENCES

The last two chapters, which discussed Hare's first book, *The Language of Morals*, can be summarized as follows. A key word is "prescribe." For Hare, to prescribe means to guide conduct by recommending, advising, resolving, commending, or in some other way telling oneself or someone else what to do. Hare applies the adjective "prescriptive" to all moral principles and all particular moral and value judgments (such as "I ought to help him" or "Running is good")—because their function is to prescribe conduct, not to describe facts, as Toulmin and other descriptivists claimed. They are really a way of telling oneself or someone else what to do.

One main purpose of *The Language of Morals* was to show how moral decision-making is a process of strict logical deduction, not some special or loose moral inference as Toulmin depicted it. Another purpose was to show that the premises from which we carry out our moral deductions must include moral principles, which are always prescriptive rather than factual.

In being non-factual, these prescriptive premises would seem to lack the certainty or firmness of factual propositions; and the conclusions we deduce from them would seem arbitrary rather than certain. Nevertheless, we saw how Hare argued at length that although they are prescriptive and non-factual, our moral principles can be well-founded and unarbitrary after all; and the particular moral judgments we deduce from them can therefore be well-founded and unarbitrary too. But then our conclusion at the end of the last chapter finally turned against Hare, and showed that he had indeed failed to prove this point.

Our work in this and the next chapter is already cut out for us: to find out whether in his next book, *Freedom and Reason*, Hare can recoup his apparent loss, and somehow demonstrate that we can deduce moral judgments that are certain, firm, and unarbitrary—and thereby account for ultimate justification.

* * *

In *Freedom and Reason*, Hare observes that moral reasoning has traditionally, but incorrectly, been viewed as "linear"—that is, as proceeding in a straight line from premises to a conclusion. In 1967, four years after the publication of *Freedom and Reason*, Hare articulated this thesis in his Inaugural Lecture at Oxford in the following way:

> If I may caricature this view about moral reasoning, it is something like this: the only way to reach a moral conclusion is to have some premises which cannot be doubted, and proceed by some approved and certified method of inference from them to a moral conclusion. . . . What is wrong with this

kind of reasoning is what we may call . . . its linearity. It is supposed to start from something given, and proceed in a straight line—or at any rate a line—until it arrives at the conclusion.[1]

In rejecting the idea that moral reasoning is linear, Hare seems to be contradicting what he said in *The Language of Morals*. But if we take another look, we will notice that in *The Language of Morals*, Hare did not depict moral deliberation as being necessarily linear. There is a change in emphasis from the first book to the second: In *The Language of Morals*, Hare left the impression that moral reasoning proceeds in a straight line from premises to conclusions; and in *Freedom and Reason* he stresses the non-linear structure of decision-making.

In the following passage from *Freedom and Reason*, Hare introduces his new thesis about the pattern of moral reasoning by comparing it to Popper's view of scientific reasoning:

A parallel from the philosophy of science will perhaps make this point clear. It is natural to suppose that what the scientist does is to reason from premisses, which are the data of observation, to conclusions, which are his 'scientific laws', by means of a special sort of inference called 'inductive'. Against this view, Professor Popper has forcibly argued that in science there are no inferences other than deductive; the typical procedure of scientists is to propound hypotheses, and then look for ways of testing them—i.e. experiments which, if they are false, will show them to be so. A hypothesis which, try as we may, we fail to falsify, we accept provisionally, though ready to abandon it if, after all, further experiment refutes it. . .[2]

For Popper, scientific reasoning is non-linear yet deductive. We would have to reject the premise "All men are mortal" if an experiment somehow showed Socrates to be immortal. Similarly, the scientist tests his hypotheses by seeing whether experiments can show them to be false.

> The only inferences which occur in this process are deductive ones, from the truth of certain observations to the falsity of a hypothesis. There is no reasoning which proceeds from the data of observation to the *truth* of a hypothesis. Scientific inquiry is rather a kind of *exploration*, or looking for hypotheses which will stand up to the test of experiment.[3]

Hare claims that moral reasoning likewise is deductive, yet non-linear and exploratory.

> I want to suggest that it too is a kind of exploration, and not a kind of linear inference, and that the only inferences which take place in it are deductive. What we are doing in moral reasoning is to look for moral judgements and moral principles which, when we have considered their logical consequences and the facts of the case, we can still accept.[4]

Hare is now emphasizing that moral reasoning is "exploratory" rather than linear—that it proceeds from consideration of the effects of moral conclusions to the *rejection* (or retaining) of major premises (principles). Nevertheless, this process consists of strict deductive logic, and is based on principles serving as major premises and on factual statements as minor premises. Therefore, what Hare is now saying in *Freedom and Reason* is essentially consistent with what he said in *The Language of Morals*.

Recalling our version of the manager-clerk example (early in Chapter 5), it now becomes clear that the reasoning which we depicted the manager as doing can be more accurately characterized as exploratory than linear. The manager started out tentatively with the syllogism "All tardy clerks ought to be fired; this one is tardy; therefore, he ought to be fired." When he became more aware of the consequences and other facts of the case (that firing the clerk would cause great hardship and that a car pool would get him to work on time after all), the manager realized that he could no longer assent to the conclusion "This clerk ought to be fired." From this it logically followed that he must reject at least one of the premises. The minor one, "This clerk is tardy," could not be doubted, so he had to reject the major premise, "All tardy clerks ought to be fired." Thus we saw how he replaced this principle with the revised one, "Tardy clerks ought to be fired only when kinder methods will not cure them."

Regardless of what example of moral reasoning one offers, Hare believes one will find it to be exploratory rather than linear. I will use Hare's example from *Freedom and Reason*,[5] with some modifications, to support this general claim.

Suppose a creditor, B, is owed money by A and is contemplating prosecuting and possibly jailing the debtor. If B thinks in the simple linear fashion which *The Language of Morals* seemed to suggest, he would reason something like this: "All people who won't pay their debts ought to be prosecuted. A won't pay his debt. Therefore, he ought to be prosecuted." Hardly anyone is so simplistic and unexploratory in his deliberating that he would reason in this rigid manner. In actual practice, we normally consider the consequences of our acts, e.g., what sending A to jail would involve. Although Hare does not depict B as contemplating the cost of prosecuting his debtor, in our use of his example we can well imagine that B would consider the cost of a court case.

If B found that prosecuting A would be too costly, he might decide against it. This would mean that B could not accept the conclusion of the above syllogism, "I ought to prosecute A." This in turn would mean that he could not accept the major premise, "All people who won't pay debts ought to be prosecuted." Instead, he would revise his major premise (his principle) into something like: "All creditors who can economically prosecute defaulting debtors ought to do so." (In actual practice there would be other considerations which would alter the major premise even further.) After presenting his version of this example, Hare once more compares this view of moral reasoning to scientific reasoning:

> We may carry the parallel further. Just as science, seriously pursued, is the search for hypotheses and the testing of them by the attempt to falsify their particular consequences, so morals, as a serious endeavour, consists in the search for principles and the testing of them against particular cases. Any rational activity has its discipline, and this is the discipline of moral thought: to test the moral principles that suggest themselves to us by following out their consequences and seeing whether we can accept *them*.[6]

TO CHECK CONSEQUENCES, WE MUST CONSIDER BEING IN THE OTHER'S SHOES

This revised account of moral reasoning leads to an answer to the lengthy objection given at the end of the last chapter, which was as follows: For Hare, moral principles, which always play a significant role in moral deductions, are non-factual, and therefore somewhat arbitrary. Accordingly, the moral conclusions we deduce from them must be somewhat arbitrary also.

To show why this objection does not stand up, let us now use the creditor-debtor example more in the way Hare does. Suppose that all of B's selfish interests incline him to jail A. That is, assume that B has no selfish reasons, such as saving court costs, to refrain from prosecuting A. Assume also (as Hare does when he presents this example) that there is another creditor, C, to whom B himself owes money, and that the amounts of money and other relevant conditions are essentially the same.

Let B's reasoning be represented by this syllogism: "All defaulting debtors ought to be jailed. A is a defaulting debtor. Therefore A ought to be jailed." B can test his major premise by replacing the statements about A with statements about B, himself. This substituting is possible because, like A, B also shares the characteristic which is relevant in this situation, namely, being a defaulting debtor. He would come up with a syllogism like this: "All defaulting debtors ought to be jailed. B is a defaulting debtor. Therefore, B ought to be jailed." B would have to accept this unpleasant conclusion about himself because it follows perfectly logically from the premises.

Suppose that B does not want to be jailed and therefore rejects the conclusion "B ought to be jailed." It would follow logically that he must also reject one of the two premises. The minor premise (B is a defaulting debtor) is factually true. Therefore, he must reject the major premise, i.e., the principle that defaulting debtors ought to be jailed.

Suppose B used his imagination and tried to visualize

what would happen if the tables were turned in this way. Unless he was eccentric, he would probably decide quickly that he could not assent to the conclusion that C should jail him. And rejecting this conclusion would also mean rejecting the *principle* that creditors ought to jail debtors, and replacing it with something else—e.g., "Creditors ought not to jail debtors." From this new principle a new conclusion would also logically follow, viz., that he (B) ought not to jail A.

We can now see more clearly what Hare is driving at: that we test our principles and acts not by narrowly thinking about our own immediate case, but by opening our minds to the other ramifications of our principles. Again, if I were B, I should not only consider whether A's being jailed would satisfy my own immediate desires; I should also consider the other consequences of my principle. Doing so would lead me to see that logically I must either assent to having myself jailed, or assent to a new and different principle, such as, Creditors ought not to jail debtors.

The exploratory use of logic—testing principles by checking the acceptability of their consequences—is now seen to have broader application. Instead of merely checking the consequences close at hand—e.g., whether I will gain financially by jailing A—one has not really tested a principle until he has considered its other logical consequences. I have not adequately tested the principle that creditors ought to jail debtors until I have considered its implication—that C jail his debtor, B, myself. Similarly, the manager should also have tested the principle "Tardy clerks ought to be fired" by considering whether he could agree that he himself ought to be fired if he had been a tardy clerk in a similar situation. And if

I am tempted to discriminate against a black person, I should test the principle "It is proper to discriminate against black people" by asking myself whether I can accept the logical consequence "I should be discriminated against" when I imagine my own skin being black.

MUST ONE FACE THE UNPLEASANT LOGICAL CONSEQUENCES?

Is it really necessary that one explore such diverse logical consequences of his principles? Why *ought* the white man pause and imagine himself in the black man's shoes? Or, does creditor B have to think about C at all? If his inclinations are to jail A, and if there is no danger of C ever hearing about the jailing of A and trying to jail B in return, can't B go ahead and jail A without thinking about what C ought to do?

Of course, B may be able physically and psychologically to close his mind and think, "I don't care about logic. I feel like jailing A, so I will." But in doing so, he would not be carrying on *moral reasoning* or moral discourse. If B does not have any thoughts such as "I *ought* to jail A" or "It is right in this situation for me to jail A," but instead thinks only, "I want to jail A and I will," and immediately files a complaint with the court, such impulsive and unreflective thinking is not what most of us call moral thinking. It surely is not the kind of thinking Hare is concerned with in his books; for a major conclusion of the last chapter was that moral reasoning involves not only singular prescriptions, such as "Let me jail A," but also *principles*.

We can also see now that thinking in terms of principles means thinking *universally*. Assenting to the principle "Creditors ought to jail debtors" entails assenting to having *all* creditors jail their debtors. Or, to agree to the principle that blacks ought to be discriminated against entails agreeing to having oneself discriminated against if one were black. In other words, whenever a person makes a serious moral assertion and says that act X is right or ought to be done, he is saying that it is right for acts of a certain *type* to be done. But this means that it is right that all acts of that type be done. Although the class may be very small, e.g., firing clerks only under conditions a, b, and c, we are still dealing with a universal principle since it pertains to *all* acts in the class. As Hare puts it briefly, "the meaning of the word 'ought' and other moral words is such that a person who uses them commits himself thereby to a universal rule."[7]

Hare calls this thesis—that a person using moral words like "ought" and "right" commits himself thereby to a universal principle—the thesis of universalizability. He elucidates it in terms of the creditor-debtor example as follows:

> B asks himself, 'Can I say that I ought to take this measure against A in order to make him pay?' He is no doubt *inclined* to do this, or *wants* to do it. Therefore, if there were no question of universalizing his prescriptions, he would assent readily to the *singular* prescription 'Let me put A into prison'. But when he seeks to turn this prescription into a moral judgement, and say, 'I *ought* to put A into prison because he will not pay me what he owes', he reflects that this would involve accepting the principle 'Anyone who is in my position ought to put his debtor into prison if he does not pay'. But then he reflects that C is in the same position of unpaid creditor with regard to himself (B), and that the cases are otherwise identical; and that if anyone in this position ought to put his debtors into prison, then so ought C to put him (B) into prison. And to

accept the moral prescription 'C ought to put me into prison' would commit him (since, as we have seen, he must be using the word 'ought' prescriptively) to accepting the singular prescription 'Let C put me into prison'; and this he is not ready to accept. But if he is not, then neither can he accept the original judgement that he (B) ought to put A into prison for debt.[8]

The answer to the question above—Can't people do what they feel like without facing the unpleasant logical consequences?—is Yes. But in doing so they are also closing their minds to thoughts about what is right or ought to be done. On the other hand, if they think in terms of right and wrong, they will also be trying to think logically, i.e., in terms of universal principles. This will mean facing the fact that their principles apply to themselves in the same way they apply to others.

Even if the agent is not literally in the same predicament as the other fellow, the way B is, he can *imagine* he is. Although a white man is not black and so vulnerable to racial prejudice, he can imagine that he is black. If he assents to the principle that blacks ought to be discriminated against, he logically must also assent to the conclusion that he himself be discriminated against if he were black.

If the white man does not assent to this unpleasant conclusion (and few if any whites would), he is logically bound to reject the principle that blacks should be discriminated against. He will, in turn, logically have to reject the particular prescription that he discriminate against a black individual whom he is tempted to discriminate against.

THE CERTAINTY OF MORAL JUSTIFICATION IS LOGICAL, NOT JUST FACTUAL

We are finally in a position to see clearly why moral conclusions can have at least as much certainty as factual propositions can. If one rejects a particular prescription, such as "Let C jail me for not paying my debt," there will be some principles which he *logically must* reject also, for example, "Creditors ought always to jail defaulting debtors." To put it a little differently, when my desires or other inclinations are such that I reject certain particular prescriptions (such as that I should be discriminated against if I were black) I will *logically have to* reject certain principles too—for example, that blacks ought to be discriminated against. It will then follow that I will be logically bound to reject other particular prescriptions, such as that I discriminate against Jones, who is black.

The necessity to accept or reject a principle does not depend on an endless chain of prior principles as suggested in the last chapter. Rather, many of the agent's principles follow with strict logical necessity from something close at hand, namely, his rejection of particular prescriptions such as "Let C jail me." Since it is logical necessity which binds the agent to choose one principle over another, the resulting prescriptive conclusion is in no sense more arbitrary than factual propositions.

Admittedly, this has been an account of how we must *reject* principles rather than accept them. But when one is confronted with a moral choice, he cannot escape making some decision. Therefore, rejecting certain principles and acts amounts to accepting others. And it will become clearer in the next chapter how this explanation in terms of testing and rejecting principles and particular prescriptions applies to moral decisions in everyday situations.

The important point at hand, though, is that Hare has finally demonstrated that one's choice of moral principles is not any more arbitrary than one's acceptance of factual propositions. Since the justification Hare has demonstrated is a function of logic and the law of contradiction, it seems to involve an even greater degree of objectivity, firmness, or certainty than do factual propositions. Thus, it seems that Hare may finally have shown how moral justification can, in the fullest sense of the word, be ultimate.

NOTES

[1] Hare, "The Practical Relevance of Philosophy" in *Essays on Philosophical Method*, p. 104.
[2] Hare, *Freedom and Reason*, p. 87.
[3] *Ibid.*, p. 88.
[4] *Ibid.*
[5] *Ibid.*, p. 90.
[6] *Ibid.*, p. 92.
[7] *Ibid.*, p. 30.
[8] *Ibid.*, p. 91.

VIII

Hare's *Freedom and Reason* (Continued): The Role of Inclinations in Justification

To fill some gaps in our understanding of the process of justification, this chapter will focus on the role of inclinations in decision-making. Since Hare's theory is very similar to Kant's, we will begin by pointing out certain similarities and differences between the two theories.

THE FACTORS RELEVANT TO FORMULATING A PRINCIPLE ARE THOSE USED IN THE ORIGINAL JUDGMENT

One objection which will probably arise from the foregoing outline of Hare's account of ultimate justification is this: An agent can often find features in himself or his situation which are distinctive, and can claim that principles which apply to another person do not quite apply to himself.

A white person might "agree in general" with the principle that people ought not to be excluded from neighborhoods because of differences in race or color. But if the white person hears that a black family is actually planning to buy the house next door, he may begin to find excuses for believing that the principle does not apply in his case. He might think, "Someone in my profession must pay special attention to who his neighbors are," or "My children are very impressionable, and I hear that the children in this black family have gotten into a lot of trouble." Similarly, Hare says of B: "He might allege, for example, that, whereas his family would starve if C put him into prison, this would not be the case if he put A into prison, because A's family would be looked after by A's relatives."[1]

Is there anything in Hare's system to prevent the agent from focusing on peculiarities of his situation in such a self-serving way? It will not do to insist that the agent ignore the details of a situation and think only in terms of very general principles, such as "*All* unpaying debtors ought to be jailed" or "Lying is *always* wrong." A common criticism of Kant's theory has been that he went to this latter extreme and expected the agent to think in terms of very general principles. According to these critics, Kant should have advised us to consider more details of the case at hand than he did. According to many, Kant should have acknowledged that it is permissible, and indeed one's duty, to lie to a would-be murderer if one thinks such a lie could prevent a crime. David Ross comments on this example and on Kant's failure to give us any means of knowing which features of a situation are to be considered:

> If C tells a lie to the would-be murderer, this falls (i) under the sub-species 'lies told to murderous persons', (ii) under the species 'lies', (iii) under the genus 'statements'. Kant pitches, arbitrarily, on the middle one of these three classes....
>
> The test of universalizability applied at one level of abstractness condemns the act; applied at another level of abstractness

it justifies it. And since the principle itself does not indicate at what level of abstractness it is to be applied, it does not furnish us with a criterion of the correctness of maxims.[2]

Can Hare give us a way to decide what is the proper level of abstractness, or which features of a situation to take into account? Yes, and he does so rather simply: Features are to be taken into account which are *relevant*; and by "relevant" Hare means those which constituted the basis of the agent's judgment in the first place. The fact that A's relatives can provide for his family if he goes to jail could have been considered relevant by B after all. When deliberating whether to jail A, B might have thought to himself, "If a debtor refuses to pay a debt *and if* his family won't starve while he is in jail, his creditor ought to jail him." If this was the principle which B expressed to himself, he was using both the factor of being a debtor *and* the factor of the family being fed as grounds for his original judgment. He was considering both factors to be relevant when deciding on his principle.

But assenting to a principle like this means assenting to having it applied universally. This in turn means that the agent must be willing to make the same judgment (He ought to be jailed) about anyone who is like the original subject (A) in relevant respects. If B found out that relatives would provide for his own family too, he would be like A in the relevant respects—having relatives to look after his family and being in debt (to C). It would follow that the original judgment, "He ought to go to jail," would apply to himself, B, as well as to A. Hare formulates these ideas as follows:

> By calling a judgement universalizable I mean only that it logically commits the speaker to making a similar judgement

about anything which is either exactly like the subject of the original judgement or like it in the relevant respects. The relevant respects are those which formed the grounds of the original judgement.[3]

Let us change the example some and pretend that A is black, and that a friend challenges B's judgment again by saying, "Imagine that you were in A's place and that your family would be fed. Can you honestly assent to the prescription that you should be jailed?" And suppose that this time B replied, "Well, don't forget, A is just a Negro, but I am white!" Such a reply would suggest that B is trying to smuggle in skin color as a relevant feature, but let's see whether he could get away with such a maneuver:

> Suppose that B alleges that the fact that A has a hooked nose or a black skin entitles him, B, to put him in prison, but that C ought not to do the same thing to him, B, because his nose is straight and his skin white. Is this an argument of equal logical respectability? Can I say that the fact that I have a mole in a particular place on my chin entitles me to further my own interests at others' expense, but that they are forbidden to do this by the fact that they lack this mark of natural pre-eminence?
> . . . all we have to do is to imagine an identical case in which the roles are reversed. Suppose that my mole disappears, and that my neighbour grows one in the very same spot on his chin. Or, to use our other example, what does B say about a hypothetical case in which he has a black skin or a hooked nose, and A and C are both straight-nosed and white-skinned?[4]

As this passage shows, even if B *did* use skin color as part of the grounds for his original judgment, he can still test his reasoning by imagining himself in A's place. In other words, suppose that when making his original judgment, he used blackness as a factor by thinking, "If a man refuses to pay a debt, has relatives to take care of his family, and is black, then he ought to be jailed." He could test this principle by imagining not only that he has relatives to feed his family but also that he is black. To be able logically to retain his principle, he would have to think something like this: "I admit that I am refusing to pay my debt to C. But even if my family would be fed, I cannot assent to C jailing me. However, when I picture myself as black, I *can* assent to C jailing me for not paying my debt." Unless B is very eccentric, it is unlikely that he would honestly think this way—that he would want his skin color to determine that he should go to jail.

Accordingly, unless B has very unusual inclinations, if he sincerely imagines himself in A's place as just described, he would probably find out that he cannot consider skin color to be a relevant feature in this situation.

In general, we often pretend that some factor such as skin color is a relevant basis for making a judgment about others but not about ourselves; but after imagining ourselves in the other's place, we may find that we cannot honestly consider that factor to be relevant. Thus, this method of imagining ourselves in the other's place seems to be a satisfactory means of deciding which features are relevant and, therefore, which factors to include in formulating our principles.

OUR INCLINATIONS DETERMINE WHAT CONSEQUENCES WE WILL PUT UP WITH

It must be emphasized that it is purely up to the individual which factors he is going to regard as relevant—skin color, the hardship of jail, concern over feeding his family, or whatever. We must understand clearly that Hare does not think that the situation itself somehow determines which considerations are morally relevant. A philosopher who says that the situation itself objectively determines what factors are relevant is espousing a form of descriptivism. He is saying that facts entail a moral conclusion. Suppose a philosopher says that blackness cannot be grounds for my excluding someone from my neighborhood even if I am willing to have myself excluded if I were black, and that the black person's being law abiding, well-mannered, and neat *are* grounds for his being accepted. The philosopher would be claiming that these facts about the black person entail that I ought to accept him. He would be a descriptivist because he would be deriving an "ought" from an "is."

Hare, on the contrary, firmly denies that the factual nature of a situation can obligate an agent to accept certain features as relevant and therefore to adopt certain principles as right. Rather, the agent may accept *any* features of the situation as morally relevant as long as he can honestly accept the logical consequences of his decision.

Since so much depends on whether the agent assents to this or that logical consequence, the question naturally arises, What determines whether he assents or not? It was simply A's *inclinations* which moved him to balk at the alternative of going to jail. In general we can say that it is one's desires or other inclinations which lead him initially to reject those logical consequences regarding himself being jailed, discriminated against, or whatever. In Hare's words, "If a man is to be compelled to a moral conclusion, he must assent to, or be unable to assent to,

Hare's Freedom and Reason (Continued) 125

certain singular prescriptions (and this will depend on what desires he has)."[5]

It can be seen that for Hare inclinations play an extremely important role, certainly more than for Kant. Kant did not have much place for inclinations in his moral system except in a negative way, as forces which tempt us to be unrational. But Hare states very explicitly and emphatically that it is inclinations which render a person willing or unwilling to assent to certain singular prescriptions so that he is logically required to reject certain principles.

Without inclinations, one would never be moved to reject any singular prescriptions and would never be required in turn by logic to reject any universal ones. He would be willing to have himself jailed, discriminated against, etc. Then he could logically assent to the principle that unpaying debtors be jailed, blacks be discriminated against, and so on. It is only because of our inclinations that we are against certain undesirable things happening to us and that we can in turn be logically required to reject certain principles. Thus, we see that inclinations play a role in Hare's system which is just as central as the role of facts and logic.

Hare summarizes this point by stating that, in addition to facts and logic,

> inclination gives us the third necessary ingredient in the argument: if B were a completely apathetic person, who literally did not mind what happened to himself or to anybody else, the argument would not touch him. The three necessary ingredients which we have noticed, then, are (1) facts; (2) logic; (3) inclinations. These ingredients enable us, not indeed to arrive at an evaluative conclusion, but to *reject* an evaluative proposition.[6]

HARE'S EMPHASIS ON INCLINATIONS HELPS HIM EXPLAIN PRACTICAL APPLICATION

As indicated above, when compared to Hare, Kant's attitude toward inclinations must be described as very negative. According to Kant, one should make moral decisions on the basis of reason alone; inclinations are not worthy of such a role. However, he also says that we ought to act only according to those maxims which we can *will* to become universal laws. What could determine such willing, if not inclinations?

Perhaps, as Kant claimed, sheer reason will find some maxims logically impossible to universalize, such as the maxim that we should lie. Still the universalizing of some other apparently immoral practices would *not* lead to logical contradiction, e.g., jailing defaulting debtors, summarily firing tardy clerks, discriminating against blacks, and many other forms of selfish and cruel behavior. To some critics of Kant, mere reason by itself would seem unable to move us to *will* that these practices not become universal. To them, reason itself seems too abstract, empty, and formal to generate the feelings one needs to will that such practices not occur worldwide. Therefore, if we relied on reason alone, we would be paralyzed when trying to make such decisions. Thus—some would object—Kant fails to explain how it is that we are able to reach moral decisions on matters of this sort.

Hare, by acknowledging the role of inclinations, clarifies how one can reach moral decisions in such concrete situations. He does not leave us with an abstract rule such as Kant's categorical imperative, which is difficult to apply in real life. Rather, he outlines a clearcut procedure which is easy to follow (assuming we have the moral resolve to do so): To tell whether I ought to do an act which I am considering (e.g., discriminating against someone), all I need to do is first check whether my prescribing the act would logically commit me to another singular prescription which I find undesirable (e.g., that I be discriminated against if I were in the other's place). Then I must imagine myself in his place to see whether I can assent to having myself suffer such consequences. If I cannot assent, then logically I must conclude that I ought not to do the act. Otherwise, it is perfectly logical for me to do it.

In short, Kant's emphasis on reason and will left many critics wondering exactly how an agent was supposed to choose one course of action over another. Hare has given a clear answer to this puzzle by explaining that inclinations make the agent unwilling to have certain things done to him, and therefore logically bound to decide against doing them to someone else in relevantly similar circumstances.

INCLINATION AND EXPLORATION HELP TO ACCOUNT FOR INDIVIDUAL CHOICE

Hare's emphasis on inclinations and on the exploratory use of logic helps to solve another puzzle: how to explain individual choice.

In Chapter 5 we observed how descriptivist theories (naturalism and intuitionism) seem unable to account for freedom of decision. According to naturalism and intuitionism, what act an agent ought to do in a given situation is determined by the factual nature of the situation. All the agent has to do is perceive or intuit accurately and reason logically; then he will *understand* what act he is to do, and presumably will do it. Thus, decision-making, as explained by descriptivist theories, seems to be an intellectual process rather than a process involving free moral choice.

Hare's account in *The Language of Morals*, and summarized above in Chapters 5 and 6, likewise depicted moral reasoning as a rigid deductive operation. *The Language of Morals* led (or at least allowed) the reader to conceive of moral reasoning as linear deduction from principles and factual minor premises. If we reconsider that account, we will notice that it also seems to allow little room for individual choice.

Let us alter Hare's "creditor" example again and suppose another creditor, Z, is in the exact same situation as B and that all of his principles which pertain to the situation happen to be identical to B's. All the major and minor premises which Z had to work with would be the same as B's. If moral reasoning were strict linear deduction, Z would inevitably end up with the same conclusions about how to act as B would.

Only in B's and Z's decisions about what principles to hold would there seem to be any factor of individual choice. However, as we saw, *The Language of Morals* depicted those decisions of principle also as being made in the very same linear deductive manner from prior principles and facts. Thus, according to our original "linear" interpretation of *The Language of Morals*, moral reasoning was such a rigidly deductive process that, as with the descriptivists and Kant, it now seems more accurate to describe it as an intellectual process than as a process involving free individual choice.

Now that we understand the role of inclinations and the exploratory use of logic, we can finally explain individual choice more satisfactorily. Even supposing

Hare's Freedom and Reason (Continued) 129

B's and Z's prior principles and the facts of their situations to be the same, Z's conclusions about how to act could still be different from B's because of a difference in his inclinations.

It is perfectly possible that Z might have a more ascetic temperament than B and would honestly be willing to undergo a term in jail if he was neglectful about repaying a loan. Consider how many of us can say, "If I were to commit murder, I ought to go to jail, and I can assent to the prescription that I be jailed if I were to commit murder." Similarly, some of us like Z might be able to say, "I ought to be jailed if I were willfully very neglectful about repaying a large loan." And the size of the debt for which various individuals would be willing to go to jail would vary with their respective temperaments or other inclinations.

Accordingly, B might not be able to assent to being jailed for a large unpaid debt and therefore rejects the principle that unpaying debtors be jailed. But suppose Z, because of different inclinations *could* assent to himself being jailed for such a debt. It would follow that, unlike B, Z would not have to reject the principle that defaulting debtors be jailed.

Hare illustrates this point as follows:

> If, on the other hand, a man says 'But I *want* to be put in prison, if ever I am in that situation', we can, indeed, get as far as accusing him of having eccentric desires; but we cannot, when we have proved to him that nobody else has such a desire, face him with the choice of either saying, with the rest, 'Let this not be done to me', or else being open to the accusation of not understanding what he is saying. For it is not an incorrect use of words to want eccentric things. . . . It is, indeed, in the logical possibility of wanting *anything* (neutrally

described) that the 'freedom' which is alluded to in my title essentially consists.[7]

Thus, how one chooses to reject, revise, or retain his principles is not determined solely by facts and his prior principles as *The Language of Morals* seemed to be saying; another major factor consists of his temperament, desires, and other inclinations. We have just seen how, because of this additional factor, two individuals can start out with the same principles in identical situations and decide on different ways of acting. What they decide is largely a function of their own feelings and individual differences. Thus, we now see how there can be much more room for the sort of thing we have been calling individual choice.

* * *

Hare also helps to account for individual choice in another way: by showing how the agent can choose from a variety of alternatives. According to our earlier linear model, the agent is bound to accept whatever principle or maxim follows logically from his prior principles and the facts of the case. According to the exploratory model, the agent is bound only to *reject* certain logically unacceptable principles and maxims. He is then perfectly free to choose any of the other logically compatible alternatives. For example, suppose that B could not assent to being jailed for a debt like A's, but could assent to being sued, having his credit rating lowered, having his employer notified, and being nagged by a bill collector. It would then be perfectly consistent of B (other things being equal) to use any one of these measures against A which he felt like using.

Thus, according to the theory in *Freedom and Reason*, our decision-making is not locked into a narrow syllogistic pattern. We are not limited to those courses of action to which deduction from principles and facts would lead us. Rather, the function of deductive logic is merely to eliminate those alternatives which lead to contradiction. And such logically unacceptable alternatives are usually few in number. This leaves us free to select any of the remaining options we happen to prefer.

To conclude, Hare has helped to explain freedom of decision by showing how there can be considerable leeway in choosing alternatives and also, as we saw a little earlier, by showing how one's own individual temperament and inclinations function to make his choices peculiar to himself.

VARIATIONS IN INCLINATIONS NEED NOT LEAD TO DISORDER IN SOCIETY

Before we return to the issue of ultimate justification, there is one more problem which, if left unattended, could make Hare's system seem so impractical, or even so dangerous, that his account of ultimate justification would appear useless. As seen in the last section, one's principles and maxims can vary with one's inclinations. It may be objected that Hare's theory thereby paves the way for anarchy in society. If there were a lot of Z's around, they could logically proceed to jail the A's. Other individuals who, because of extreme masochism, death instinct, or suicidal tendencies could assent to having themselves murdered, would find it permissible to murder others. And men who (because of their inclinations) could assent to the prescription that they be raped if they were women would find it moral to rape women. In general, it would seem that whoever had eccentric or perverted inclinations would find it morally justifiable to inflict his perversions on others.

One answer which Hare has to this objection is that although differences in inclinations will often lead people to choose different courses of action, these disagreements will not usually be harmful or disruptive. The reason is that people's inclinations do not vary enough to lead to much conflict—as long as the individuals make sure they can universalize their maxims. As Hare says, "People's inclinations about most of the important matters in life tend to be the same (very few people, for example, like being starved or run over by motorcars)."[8]

Thus, although Hare's acknowledgement of the role of inclinations and the exploratory use of logic does account for individuality in moral decision-making, the variations from one agent to the next will hardly ever be enough to undermine productive moral discourse, and certainly not enough to lead to anarchy in society.

In the second half of *Freedom and Reason*, Hare elaborates on his doctrine about the role of inclinations by pointing out that although variations in inclinations can lead to legitimate differences in opinion, this does not mean that an agent ought to be concerned only about his *own* inclinations. The agent often has to take account of the other party's feelings. Hare makes this very clear with the following example:

> A likes to listen to classical chamber music on his gramophone, and B, who lives in the next room, is considering whether to practice playing jazz on the trumpet. Now it is obviously of no

Hare's Freedom and Reason (Continued) 133

use for B to ask himself whether he is prepared to prescribe universally that people should play trumpets when they live next door to other people who are listening to classical records. For if B himself were listening to classical records (which bore him beyond endurance) he would be only too pleased if somebody next door started up on the trumpet.[9]

If B is going to imagine himself in A's place in a meaningful way, he must imagine himself as having A's taste for classical music. He would think, "When I imagine listening to classical music and enjoying it, I cannot assent to the proposition that a neighbor should blast me out with his trumpet."

Thus, it is clear that universalizing one's prescriptions and imagining oneself in the other person's place entails making allowances for the other's tastes and feelings. Suppose B were to ignore his neighbor's feelings and think, "If I were in my neighbor's place, I would enjoy hearing the trumpet, and the fact that my neighbor dislikes hearing it doesn't matter to me." He would be operating on the principle that people ought to *ignore* others' likes and dislikes. It would logically follow that people ought to ignore his (B's) likes and dislikes also. B probably could not agree to having others disregard how he feels; therefore, to be logical, he must not disregard how others feel either. As Hare expresses it,

> the natural way for the argument then to run is for B to admit that he is not prepared to prescribe universally that people's likes and dislikes should be disregarded by other people, because this would entail prescribing that other people should disregard his own likes and dislikes.[10]

How much weight should be assigned to the individual interests of the various parties, e.g., how loud and how long A and B should play their jazz and classical music respectively, is a complicated problem which Hare discusses to some extent in his chapter on utilitarianism, but which we do not need to get into here.

The only point which we are concerned with now is that even where there is considerable variation in people's tastes and other feelings, it does not necessarily follow that their decisions about how to act will conflict. Rather, if one wants to have his feelings regarded by other people, he is bound by logic to regard their feelings also. With this general insight, it should be fairly clear that regard for others' feelings can lead to agreement in most situations.

FANATICS ESCAPE CENSURE. IS THIS A FLAW IN HARE'S THEORY?

Oddly enough there may be some individuals whose inclinations are so eccentric that they *can* assent to having their feelings disregarded. Hare calls them fanatics and shows how our trumpeter could become such a fanatic if his affection for the instrument were so great as to be an "ideal":

> Suppose that B says, 'I am not, indeed, prepared to prescribe universally that people's likes and dislikes should be disregarded by other people; but I *am* prepared to prescribe universally that they should be disregarded under a certain specified condition, viz. when they interfere with the playing of the trumpet—that noble instrument'. If B takes this line, he is displaying more than a mere inclination to play the trumpet...
> B will only take the line suggested if he has, not a mere inclination, but what we shall later call an ideal. That is to say, he must be, not merely wanting to play the trumpet himself,

Hare's Freedom and Reason (Continued) 135

> but thinking it good that the trumpet should be played by whomsoever, and that whosoever plays it should not be frustrated, even by B himself if he has become so depraved as to lose his taste for the instrument.[11]

In fact, some fanatics may be so dedicated to an ideal that they will espouse it at the cost of great suffering to themselves or even their own death.

However, most people who appear to act fanatically are not true fanatics. Hare's device of testing one's principles by checking the acceptability of the logical consequences can be used on them. This device can lead them to see that they were treating as relevant some feature of a situation which, upon closer analysis, they cannot hold as relevant.

For example, Hare shows how, if we could get a Nazi who believes in killing Jews to talk with us enough, we might test him so that either of two things would happen. (1) We would find out that he is indeed a true fanatic who will die for his principle that all Jews ought to be exterminated; or (2) we could get him to admit that race is irrelevant to one's right to live:

> We say to him 'You may not know it, but we have discovered that you are not the son of your supposed parents, but of two pure Jews; and the same is true of your wife'; and we produce apparently cast-iron evidence to support this allegation. Is he at all likely to say—as he logically *can* say—'All right then, send me and all my family to Buchenwald!'?[12]

We can probably rest assured that with this test most Nazis would turn out to be less than true fanatics, and rather than die would give up their principle that Jews be exterminated. In other words, if we could talk with them along enough to get them to vividly imagine themselves being Jews, they would acknowledge that they could not agree to their being killed for their Jewishness. Thus, Hare's method of argument would have worked in the case of these unauthentic fanatics.

It now becomes even more evident how basically similar almost everyone's inclinations are. They are similar enough so that if Hare's procedure of exploring the logical implications of one's prescriptions were carried out thoroughly, almost no one would end up prescribing acts which would significantly undermine the happiness and health of society.

Nevertheless, there still seem to be hard-core fanatics who are truly willing to die for their ideal. In this category may be some of the recent airplane hijackers and other terrorists who belong to certain fanatical political groups or religious sects. Hare admits that his theory does not provide a way to argue with such people and show them that they are wrong.

Is this a weakness in his theory? Is the purpose of moral philosophy to prove that everyone ought to act a certain way in a given situation? Or is its purpose merely to help people to think clearly so that most of them can agree on principles which can reconcile conflicting interests justly? Hare reflects on these questions:

> That there will always be fanatics must be admitted; but it can also be admitted that the true fanatics are relatively few, and would have no power at all to do harm, were it not for their ability to mislead, and thus win the support of, large numbers of people who are not themselves fanatics. This they do by concealing facts and spreading falsehoods; by arousing passions which will cloud the sympathetic imagination—in short by all the familiar methods of propaganda. These methods would have less power over people if one essential condition for their success were removed: confused thinking. If a person

understands clearly what he is doing when he is asking a moral question and answering it. . . then the propagandist will have little power over him. To arm people in this way against propaganda is the function of moral philosophy.[13]

We have reached the end of our presentation of Hare's ethical theory, so a very brief recapitulation is in order. To the objection that there must be something wrong with Hare's theory if it cannot censure the true fanatic, Hare has answered that an ethical theory is not intended to censure everyone who deviates from society's norms. Rather, the function of moral philosophy is to facilitate productive moral thinking and discourse.

Furthermore, Hare seems to have accounted for ultimate justification. He has demonstrated how we can be *required* to do or not to do certain acts: Whenever an agent is unwilling to have a particular kind of act done against him, he is bound by the logic of his own decision-making to conclude that he ought not to do that sort of act against someone else. If I am unwilling to be discriminated against in situation x, y, z, there are no if's and's and but's about it: insofar as I think logically, I *cannot* avoid the conclusion that I ought not to discriminate against someone else in such a situation. There is no point in asking for further reasons why I must not discriminate. The conclusion that I ought not to discriminate is fully justified; my conclusion that I ought not to discriminate in this instance is proven.

A NOTE ABOUT HARE'S OTHER BOOKS

Although we have spent four chapters on Hare, it is not our purpose in this book to present a complete or balanced survey of his ethical theory. Our purpose is to find an account of ultimate justification. We have selected two of Hare's books, *The Language of Morals* and *Freedom and Reason*, to focus on, because they give the clearest presentation of the ideas needed for our project.

Before leaving these four chapters on Hare, the reader will be better oriented if Hare's other books are at least mentioned. In addition to *The Language of Morals* and *Freedom and Reason*, in 1971 and 1972 Hare published four volumes of his papers. His newest book is *Plato*, and his one remaining book is *Moral Thinking: Its Levels, Method, and Point*.[14]

Although a discussion of *Moral Thinking* would not have fit very well into the plan of this book, some readers will be especially interested in obtaining it because it has much to say about ethical theory that is very important. It is largely an elaboration and deepening of the ideas which Hare developed in *The Language of Morals* and *Freedom and Reason* and which we have already discussed.

Also, *Moral Thinking* provides further explanation as to why Hare's ethical system deals adequately with the fanatic. I argued above that Hare handles the fanatic problem in a way that gives a complete account of ultimate justification. But *Moral Thinking* discusses the fanatic in more depth—although in a rather complicated way which we will not attempt to work into this book. Nevertheless, despite what I consider to be a successful resolution of the fanatic problem, Hare's treatment of it (including that given in *Moral Thinking*) *can* be viewed as a weakness of his system. Our next chapter will address this alleged weakness and will offer an approach to it which will help to round out our account of ultimate justification.

NOTES

[1] *Freedom and Reason*, p. 106.
[2] Sir David Ross, *Kant's Ethical Theory* (Oxford: The Clarendon Press, 1954), p. 32–33.
[3] *Freedom and Reason*, p. 139.
[4] *Ibid.*, p. 106–7.
[5] *Ibid.*, p. 198.
[6] *Ibid.*, p. 92.
[7] *Ibid.*, p. 110.
[8] *Ibid.*, p. 97.
[9] *Ibid.*, p. 112.
[10] *Ibid.*, p. 113.
[11] *Ibid.*, p. 114.
[12] *Ibid.*, p. 171.
[13] *Ibid.*, p. 185.
[14] For the reader's convenience I will list all eight of Hare's books. R. M. Hare, *The Language of Morals* (Oxford: Oxford University Press, 1952); *Freedom and Reason* (Oxford: Oxford University Press, 1963); *Practical Inferences* (Berkeley: University of California Press, 1971); *Essays on Philosophical Method* (Berkeley: University of California Press, 1971); *Essays on the Moral Concepts* (Berkeley: University of California Press, 1972); *Applications of Moral Philosophy* (Berkeley: University of California Press, 1972); *Moral Thinking: Its Levels, Method, and Point* (Oxford: Oxford University Press, 1981); *Plato* (Oxford: Oxford University Press, 1982). *Practical Inferences* contains a complete bibliography of Hare's works up to 1971, and *Moral Thinking* gives a complete bibliography from 1971 to 1981.

Part Three

Completing the Account of Ultimate Justification

IX

Building on Hare With Help From Gewirth

In light of the foregoing analysis, we can consider Hare's ethical theory to provide a complete and satisfactory account of ultimate justification. Nevertheless, its difficulty in censuring the true fanatic still bothers some critics. Although this difficulty is not a weakness in the account of ultimate justification per se, it can be viewed as a weakness in Hare's theory of ethics in general. This may cause some readers also to feel dissatisfied with the account of ultimate justification which we have discovered within Hare's ethical theory.

"Fanatics can 'get away with murder' under Hare's system. Surely a moral theory should be able to tell anyone who is committing murder that he is wrong," say the critics. "Consider the recent rise in hijacking, bombing, and other terrorist activities being performed in the name of political and religious ideals: it is now more important than ever that we have grounds for declaring such behavior morally wrong," critics might add. To satisfy them, let us see whether we can amend Hare's theory so that it can readily censure the true fanatic. If we can, our account of ultimate justification will probably be more acceptable to many readers.

Imagine for a moment that there are no true fanatics in the world. That is, suppose that no human being could ever willingly sacrifice his life for the sake of an ideal such as Nazism. What we are imagining is that all of us, including all Nazis and other fanatics, have some overriding inclination which makes us unwilling to suffer death for the sake of any ideal. If this were so, it would seem that every human being—fanatics and the rest—would be required by logic always to decide against inflicting such harm on others. And Hare's fanatic problem would be eliminated.

Although Hare does not think there is any such overriding inclination, writings of a few other philosophers, especially Alan Gewirth (b. 1912), suggest that there may be.[1] Making use of Gewirth's insight, we shall develop a thesis which is partially based on Gewirth's analysis and which provides a useful approach to Hare's fanatic problem, as well as a valuable new dimension to our account of ultimate justification.

ONE THING NO ONE WILL EVER GIVE UP IS "IMMEDIATE FREEDOM"

In instances where a person does an act involuntarily or unthinkingly, it is likely that he does not want to do the act, or that he feels neutral about it. If a person performs an act voluntarily, he must have a "pro-attitude" toward it. For, if the agent acts freely and purposively, he necessarily favors his doing the act or else he would not bother to do it. Using Hare's terminology, if an agent chooses to do an act, he must at that moment be *prescribing* that he do it.

It is also clear that if an agent prescribes his doing an act at a given moment, he must at that moment be against having anything prevent him from doing it. That is, he

Building on Hare With Help From Gewirth 145

must be prescribing that he be able to do the act, i.e., that he be free to do it. For example, even if a Nazi chose to give up his life for his ideal, he would not be giving up his freedom to do the thing he was immediately deciding to do, namely, to die for Nazism. In choosing Nazism over his own life, he would be exercising and appreciating his freedom to carry out what he was choosing to do. He would be expecting and prescribing for himself the opportunity to have the fate he was selecting—death for the sake of Nazism.

I will use the term "immediate freedom" for freedom to do what one is now choosing. It must be contrasted with what may be called one's "future prerogatives." People sometimes voluntarily give up their future prerogatives. The Nazi fanatic who finds out he is Jewish might very well turn himself over to the authorities so that they can make all future decisions about what he is to do. In voluntarily giving himself up the Nazi fanatic would be expecting and prescribing that he be free to do the very thing he is *now* choosing—namely, to turn himself over to the authorities. If a friend (or "deprogrammer") found him on his way to the Nazi headquarters and kidnapped him to prevent him from throwing away his future, the Nazi fanatic would feel frustrated and angry (assuming that he was sincerely committed to turning himself over to the authorities).

In general then, every agent, including Hare's fanatic, necessarily values and prescribes his own immediate freedom in an overriding way. Although one may value some ideal more than his own life or pleasure, he will never value the ideal more than his own freedom to do what he is presently choosing. For choosing to promote an ideal presupposes exercising, appreciating, and thus prescribing the freedom to promote it.

LOGIC REQUIRES US TO PRESCRIBE OTHERS' FREEDOM AS WELL AS OUR OWN

It may be inappropriate to classify this prescribing of immediate freedom as an inclination, but it functions as we suggested an overriding inclination might function. Since no one will give up his immediate freedom for an ideal or anything else, no one will assent to having others take away that freedom. All of us inevitably prescribe our own immediate freedom; but in doing so, we are also prescribing that nothing thwart that freedom—including other people.

Now we can apply Hare's thesis of universalizability and make the following observation: Since all agents inevitably are unwilling to have anyone thwart their immediate freedom, they are required by logic not to decide to thwart the immediate freedom of others.

In this and any other application of the thesis of universalizability, Hare would want us to keep in mind the question of relevant similarity. Logic requires the agent not to decide to thwart another person's freedom only if he and the other person are similar in all relevant respects. Remember, a "relevant respect" is any feature of the parties or situation which the agent uses as a basis for his decision. If the Nazi fanatic claims that Jewishness is grounds for killing a Jew and is willing to be killed if he turned out to be Jewish, then he is consistently using Jewishness as a basis for his decision. And Jewishness is a relevant criterion as he makes his decision whether to kill the Jew.[2]

However, no agent can consistently claim that race or anything else is a relevant feature when it comes to deciding whether to undermine someone else's freedom. To do so, the agent would have to assent to the denial of

Building on Hare With Help From Gewirth 147

his own freedom of the present moment if he turned out to have the other person's race (or whatever the quality might be). But the agent will not assent to this freedom being denied; for, in making his decision about whether to interfere with the other person's freedom, the agent would be exercising and appreciating his own immediate freedom, and thereby prescribing that it *not* be denied.[3]

To return to the main point, every agent is logically required to prescribe other people's freedom, just as he prescribes his own. This requirement is a result of logic plus his inevitable valuing of his own freedom. In short, because every agent prescribes that he be free to act as he sees fit, he is logically required to prescribe that others have similar freedom.

To summarize briefly, we seem to have found a way out of Hare's fanatic problem. Thanks to insights of a few other philosophers, especially Gewirth, we have found something which functions as if it were an overriding inclination: No one, not even the fanatic, can assent to the loss of his immediate freedom to do what he is choosing. Therefore, even the fanatic is required by logic to conclude that he ought to avoid acts (e.g., murder or hijacking) which would thwart others' immediate freedom.

WE WILL GIVE UP FUTURE PREROGATIVES BUT NOT OUR IMMEDIATE FREEDOM

This addition to Hare's theory must quickly be defended against certain objections. First, is it really true that no one at all can assent to the loss of his immediate freedom? Let's take a harder look to see whether a thoroughly committed fanatic couldn't somehow choose to give up his immediate freedom in order to promote his ideal.

Picture a passionately fanatical Nazi who finds out that he is Jewish. He immediately marches to the nearest Nazi headquarters and turns himself in. Instead of saying, "Kill me," he says to the authorities, "Do with me whatever you wish—torture me, parade me in front of others to serve as an example, or whatever you want." He is such an ardent Nazi that he wants to let the authorities decide what to do with him. Isn't he thereby giving up his immediate freedom?

No. What he is giving up is his future prerogatives. He is choosing to have the authorities begin managing his life at a particular time in the future. In his case, that particular time happens to be only a few minutes or even a few seconds from the present moment. Even so, he is not giving up his immediate freedom.

Immediate freedom is the freedom, leeway, latitude, or non-interference one needs to carry out whatever at the present moment he is intending to carry out. It is the condition of not having anyone or anything block or interfere with his doing or achieving what he presently is choosing to do or achieve.

According to our example, what the fanatic is presently choosing is to carry out his Nazi duty by informing the authorities of his Jewishness and by offering to have them manage his life. If someone interferes with *this* immediate goal, he would indeed feel frustrated—assuming he is the sort of true, devoted Nazi depicted in our example.

In this example, we are assuming that our Jewish Nazi is such a fanatic that he genuinely wants the authorities to take charge of his future as soon as possible. We are not imagining him to be a lukewarm Nazi who would tend to hide his Jewishness. Thus, if someone blocks his attempt to turn himself in, he will feel frustrated.

The point is that his immediate freedom pertains to the attaining of this goal (turning himself in). He has his mind set on achieving this short range objective. Therefore he necessarily wants the leeway, opportunity, or noninterference (i.e., immediate freedom) which will allow him to do so.

The fact that achieving this short range goal of turning himself over to the authorities will result in lack of freedom in the future (future prerogatives) does not imply that he is willing to give up immediate freedom. In fact, the more determined he is to give up future prerogatives by turning himself over to the authorities, the more carefully he will have to guard his immediate freedom. That is, if he wants to make sure to succeed in relinquishing his future prerogatives by having the authorities take him over, he will have to be careful not to have anyone interfere with his plan to go to the Nazi headquarters.

He may have to guard against being kidnapped by friends, family, or "de-programmers" who don't want him to throw his life away. Thus, the more he wants to give up his freedom of the future (future prerogatives), the more attentively he will have to guard his immediate freedom.

Even if it is now clear that our Jewish Nazi fanatic is giving up his future prerogatives rather than his immediate freedom, it is not so clear that this is the case with another type of person. As Sartre, Erich Fromm, and others have pointed out, everyone has some desire to escape from freedom; and in some individuals this desire is paramount.[4]

To take an extreme example, don't many drug addicts desperately want to sabotage their own freedom to choose what is to happen to them? And don't they want to lose this freedom as quickly as possible? Thus, it would seem as if they want to give up their immediate freedom.

On the contrary, if the addict takes a drug in order to turn himself into an object and thereby give up his own freedom, it is always his future prerogatives he is choosing to relinquish—not his immediate freedom. He is choosing to insert that needle into himself so that he will no longer be able to make choices a few seconds from now. If the needle breaks as he is inserting it, he will be annoyed; and this shows that he wants the (immediate) freedom to do what he is now choosing—to insert the needle.

If someone comes along and tries to wrest the needle away from him, the addict will struggle to continue injecting himself. If someone knocks the needle out of his hand and runs off with all of his heroin, he will feel frustrated and angry. Like the rest of us, the addict wants to be able to carry out the immediate project which he has decided to do—even if his project is to become *un*able to carry out further projects by becoming drugged. And for him to want to be able to carry out this immediate project *is* for him to want to have his immediate freedom.

In other words, an agent may intend to lose his freedom by having a drug distort his decision-making ability very quickly. But this does not mean that the agent is willing to have that very intent frustrated. That is, I may choose to become unfree, but I still want the independence to do what will achieve that unfreedom. For example, I want the independence or immediate freedom necessary for me to accomplish my intended act of getting the needle into my arm. Thus, even if I choose to become unfree, I cherish the freedom to take the steps necessary to become unfree.

Accordingly, even in an extreme case of someone trying to escape his freedom by some quick and effective means such as taking drugs, the agent still guards and cherishes the independence (immediate freedom) needed to carry out the particular act he is presently choosing.

WE *CANNOT* GIVE UP IMMEDIATE FREEDOM: DECIDING TO ACT PRESUPPOSES IT

It is becoming evident that the reason no one will ever give up immediate freedom is that to do so would be impossible. We are constantly deciding to carry out minor acts as well as major projects—to type a page, buy a car, get married, or to help stamp out crime. When I decide to do some act or project, I am deciding to carry something out. I am deciding to achieve that goal. I am not merely deciding to decide, or deciding to begin acting, or deciding to make an attempt. I am deciding to *do* the thing. I am prescribing that I actually carry out or accomplish the act or project.

One cannot accomplish an act or project if he is prevented from doing it. Therefore, when one prescribes that he carry out a certain act, he or she necessarily is unwilling to be prevented from carrying it out. I cannot have my mind made up to type this page and at the same time be willing to be prevented from typing it. If I am willing to be prevented from typing it, then I don't have my mind entirely made up to type it.

In general, one *cannot* decide to do a given act and be willing to be prevented from doing it. If one is willing to be prevented from doing the act he has in mind, then he has not fully decided to carry out the act.

Although we often consider doing one thing or another without making our minds up fully, there are always other things that we fully make our minds up to do. My mind may not be fully made up to pursue the line of thought I am now writing about; but I have definitely decided to work on this book now. I may have my mind made up to go downstairs to eat lunch, but not be sure yet whether to make a sandwich or heat up some soup. With respect to those acts I have fully made up my mind to do, I cannot be willing to be prevented from doing them. Thus, although others can block my immediate freedom, I myself *cannot* be willing to give up this freedom to do whatever I am presently (and fully) intending to do.

Since no agent can ever willingly give up his immediate freedom, this inevitable unwillingness functions as an overriding inclination.

However, since one *cannot* give up immediate freedom, this inevitable unwillingness would seem to be unlike an ordinary inclination. It is a function of the very choosing process itself and thus in a sense is beyond the agent's control. Therefore, it might be objected that our unwillingness to give up our immediate freedom is not an inclination and therefore cannot serve the function we have claimed for it—that of an overriding inclination within the framework of Hare's ethical system.

Even if this unwillingness should not be classified as an inclination, the fact remains that every agent inevitably cherishes and guards his immediate freedom and is unwilling to have others interfere with it. Since every agent inevitably is unwilling to have his freedom interfered with by others, if he interfered with *theirs*, he would be treating them in a way that he is unwilling to have himself treated. He would be acting as if what's good for the goose is not good for the gander. Therefore, by universalizability, logic requires him not to decide to violate the immediate freedom of others.

HAVE WE DERIVED AN "OUGHT" FROM AN "IS"?

It might seem as if we have deduced an "ought" from an "is." Haven't we started out with a factual proposition, namely, "All agents are unwilling to give up their immediate freedom"? And haven't we derived an "ought," namely, "All agents ought to refrain from interfering with the freedom of others"?

Using reasoning which is rather similar to that I have presented, Alan Gewirth for one believes he has derived an "ought" from an "is." I have explained at length elsewhere why I believe Gewirth has not succeeded in this attempt;[5] and it would take us too far afield to analyze his argument here. I will merely outline very briefly why the foregoing demonstration does not yield an "ought" from an "is."

There are two parallel lines of reasoning which need to be distinguished. Someone observing or thinking *about* an agent (or the agent taking the viewpoint of observer about himself) might be depicted as going through a series of steps such as the following:

The agent is unwilling to have his immediate freedom thwarted.
Thus he prescribes that others not thwart his immediate freedom.

If he prescribes that he thwart such freedom in others, he will be inconsistent.

Therefore, logic requires him not to prescribe that he thwart others' immediate freedom.

Thus, logic requires him to conclude that he *ought* not to thwart the immediate freedom of others.

In articulating these steps, we are taking the viewpoint of outsiders or observers who are describing what is going on with the agent. All these steps are descriptive, factual propositions. The premise is a factual sentence; and the conclusion as well is a factual (or "is") proposition, stating the fact that logic requires the agent to conclude that he ought not to interfere with others' freedom. Thus, we have derived an "is" from an "is", not an "ought" from an "is."

Now let's consider the agent's viewpoint. The reasoning the agent does from his viewpoint consists of prescriptions. Although he does not normally put the steps of his reasoning into words, he reasons at least implicitly from a premise expressing his desire for freedom. That is, one of his prescriptions expresses his unwillingness to have others interfere with his freedom to do the act he is now choosing, and it might be formulated this way: "Let no one interfere with my freedom to do this act."

The agent would be contradicting himself if at the same time he prescribed that he thwart someone else's immediate freedom. Thus, because he, like all of us, inevitably holds the premise "Let no one interfere with my freedom to do this act," he is logically required to conclude, "Let me not interfere with the freedom of others."

In general, from our viewpoint as agents, all of us are logically required to arrive at the prescriptive conclusion, "Let me not interfere with the freedom of others," or to put it in more traditional moral terms, "I ought not to interfere with the freedom of others."

In pursuing this line of reasoning from the agent's viewpoint, we have not derived our "ought" conclusion from any "is." This "ought" has been derived from another "ought" or prescriptive premise—namely, the inevitable prescription which all agents hold at least implicitly: "Let no one interfere with my freedom to do this act."

Thus, from his viewpoint, the agent derives an "ought" from another prescriptive premise. But from the viewpoint of *observer*, we start out with an "is" statement *describing the fact* that the agent (or every agent) inevitably prescribes his immediate freedom. But then we can only infer another "is" stating the fact that the agent is logically required to conclude that he ought not to thwart others' freedom. Thus, our analysis has not revealed any way of switching from a descriptive, factual premise to a prescriptive conclusion. That is, we have not derived an "ought" from an "is."

* * *

Nevertheless, it should be clear now that the agent's "ought" is as firmly established as it would have been if it had been inferred from an "is." This is so for the following reasons: The prescriptive premise it is derived from ("Let no one interfere with my freedom to do this act") is necessarily held by all agents. From this inevitable premise, all agents are required by logic to infer the "ought" conclusion ("I ought not to interfere with others' immediate freedom"). Thus, the "ought" is inescapable for everyone—even though it is not derived from an "is."

To conclude, what we have achieved seems just as worthwhile and satisfying as deriving "ought" from "is" would be. Although we have not shown how a moral "ought" can be grounded in fact, we have arrived at an "ought" which can be called firm, certain, absolute, and universal. For we have shown that every agent inevitably holds the premise that his immediate freedom not be violated. Thanks to this inescapable premise given by Gewirth and the logic mapped out by Hare, it is certain that, insofar as they think logically, all agents, even the wildest fanatics and the most slavish addicts, necessarily arrive at the conclusion "I ought not to interfere with the immediate freedom of others."

NOTES

[1] Alan Gewirth, *Reason and Morality* (Chicago: The University of Chicago Press, 1978), pp. 48 ff; "Categorial Consistency in Ethics," *The Philosophical Quarterly* 17 (1967), 289–299; "Must One Play the Moral Language Game?" *American Philosophical Quarterly* 7, no. 2 (April 1970), 107–118; "The Justification of Egalitarian Justice," *American Philosophical Quarterly* 8, no. 4 (October 1971). The others I have in mind are Lansing Pollock and John Wilson. See Lansing Pollock, "Freedom and Universalizability," *Mind* (1973), 234–48; "The Freedom Principle," *Ethics* 86, no. 4 (July 1976), 332–42; and John Wilson, "Why Should Other People Be Treated As Equals?" *Revue Internationale de Philosophie* 97 (1971), 272–86.

[2] R. M. Hare, *Freedom and Reason* (Oxford: Oxford University Press, 1952), pp. 139 f.

[3] Gewirth expresses essentially the same insight in various places. See Gewirth, *Reason and Morality*, pp. 104 f.; "Categorial Consistency in Ethics," p. 290; and "The Justification of Egalitarian Justice," pp. 338 f.

[4] Jean-Paul Sartre, *Being and Nothingness*, trans. Hazel E. Barnes (New York: Philosophical Library, 1956), pp. 47 ff.; Erich Fromm, *Escape from Freedom* (New York: Rinehart and Company, 1941), pp. 136 ff.

[5] Paul Allen III, "A Critique of Gewirth's 'Is-Ought' Derivation," *Ethics* 92, no. 2 (January 1982), 211–226; "'Ought' from 'Is'? What Hare and Gewirth Should Have Said," *American Journal of Theology and Philosophy* 3, no. 3 (September 1982), 90–97.

X

Practical Application and Summary

OUR THEORY LABELS NOTHING GOOD OR BAD BUT STILL GIVES GUIDANCE

Most ethical theories claim to establish some summum bonum, way of life, or basic principle as the right one to live by. For example, utilitarians claim that one ought to live in a way that will maximize everyone's happiness. The theory being presented here, on the contrary, is not normative. It does not construe any value or principle as good or right.

Our theory merely demonstrates that insofar as any agent is logical, he will decide against treating others in ways he is unwilling to have himself treated. It further points out—and this is the only way our theory differs from Hare's—that one thing every logical agent will decide against doing is thwarting others' immediate freedom. Our theory does not say that thwarting others' immediate freedom is *wrong*. It merely observes that, insofar as they decide logically, all agents *will conclude that* doing so is wrong.

Therefore, our theory is metaethical rather than normative. Even so, there are ways this theory can be applied in specific situations. Exactly how and to what extent one can "apply" any moral theory is itself an involved question. Suffice it to say that, as Hare has already shown us, moral reasoning is not a matter of reasoning in a straight line from premise to conclusion (for example, "One ought to maximize pleasure. Telling Jones the truth would maximize pleasure. Therefore, I ought to tell Jones the truth."). It is more a process of exploring and testing logical implications of the prescriptions we are considering acting on, until we find one which does not land us in contradiction.

Because we have already illustrated our theory with many straightforward examples, it is hardly necessary to give any more of this sort. We have discussed at length how when one is thinking of prosecuting a debtor, firing an employee, discriminating against a minority person, and so on, one may use his imagination enough to consider whether he is willing to have himself prosecuted, fired, etc. *If* he is unwilling, and if he does not deceive himself by indulging in self-contradictory thinking, he will conclude that he ought not to jail, fire (etc.) the other person.

When we are busy making an actual moral decision, we normally are not very conscious of ourselves carrying out a process of exploring and testing principles. And at this point, the morally conscientious reader may feel let down and ask, "Does this theory merely describe the reasoning I already go through anyway? Can't it *help* me make decisions and be a better person?" One answer is that although the ostensible purpose of this metaethical analysis has been to show how rational people *do* make moral decisions, the serious reader could not read at length about avoiding self-contradictory prescribing without becoming more conscious and careful about his own prescribing. Therefore, studying this theory probably will tend to make one more conscious of his moral reasoning, and more conscientious about being logically consistent.

Practical Application and Summary 161

Second, we can also apply this theory in a more deliberate manner to help us think through many of the difficult moral problems that confront us.

Suppose one is agonizing over whether to get a divorce and is concerned about the harm it would do to the children. If he makes a deliberate effort to imagine being in their place, he might see clearly that, despite the other factors favoring divorce, he cannot assent to the suffering he would go through if he were one of the children. Then logic would require that he not get the divorce.

On the other hand, he might see clearly that he (again taking the child's place) *is* willing to undergo such suffering for the sake of the benefits to the parents. Then it would not be illogical of him to decide in favor of divorce. Of course, it might seem unrealistic and simplistic to speak of deliberately applying this theory in such a complicated and emotional situation. But we must make an effort to systematize our thinking if we are to have any hope of making such decisions rationally.

Now consider an industrialist, administrator, or politician who has to decide whether to vote for or carry out a program or project which is apt to harm some people—for example, building a power plant in a populated area, instituting the military draft, or raising taxes. He can make a deliberate effort to imagine being in the other parties' places, and consider whether he is willing to undergo the inevitable hardships for the sake of the benefits that would accrue.

In the case of the draft, he might think, "I can assent to being drafted under these conditions if I were a young man because, despite the hardships involved, I am willing to make such a sacrifice." Then it would be consistent of him to go ahead and promote the draft. Or he might find that he can*not* assent to being drafted under those conditions, and logic would require him to decide against the draft.

As these examples illustrate, even though our theory is not normative, one can use it consciously and deliberately to make difficult moral decisions.

ALTHOUGH HARD CASES SPARK DEBATE, WE *HAVE* ACCOUNTED FOR ULTIMATE JUSTIFICATION

To give a thorough analysis of how this theory can be applied in real life situations, we would have to enter into a lengthy discussion of various "hard cases" and other complications. To be brief, let's limit our discussion to what seem to be the two major types of difficulties.

Because we wanted to censure the fanatic, we have added onto Hare's theory our thesis about immediate freedom: *If* I find myself tempted to interfere with someone else's immediate freedom, my inevitable unwillingness to have my own immediate freedom thwarted, plus logic, will require that I decide not to interfere with the other person's immediate freedom. However, since most of us are not fanatics, we will seldom have to focus on this addendum to Hare's theory. (In fact the last few examples did not focus on it.) In general, what the logic of moral reasoning (universalizability) requires is simply that you and I avoid prescribing for the other party whatever we are unwilling to prescribe for ourselves—be it loss of immediate freedom, death, jail, or whatever.

In fact, situations will arise where we will *necessarily* bypass the requirement regarding immediate freedom and base our reasoning directly on the wider principle of

Practical Application and Summary 163

universalizability. If a policeman grabs a mugger by surprise to block his attempt to mug a pedestrian, he will be thwarting the mugger's immediate freedom. But if he lets him continue mugging, the policeman will be interfering with the *pedestrian's* immediate freedom, because it is his role as policeman to protect people in such situations. Since the policeman would be interfering with one or the other party's immediate freedom regardless of which alternative he takes, he will have to base his decision on other relevant considerations.

For example, suppose that when the policeman imagines himself in the pedestrian's place, he is unwilling to be left undefended and that when he puts himself in the mugger's place, he thinks "I *can* assent to being apprehended if I were such a mugger because I would deserve it, and it would teach me a much needed lesson." Logic would then have him decide to arrest the mugger.

Another kind of complication which should be discussed at length, but which we will touch on only briefly here, is illustrated in the following example. Suppose you find a friend attempting suicide, and the only way to stop him is to take him by surprise and by force. Intuition will probably tell you to go ahead and use force; but our theory would seem to indicate that this would be interfering with his immediate freedom. On reflection, we may be able to justify using force in this instance on grounds that your friend's attempt to commit suicide is a result of confusion about what he is really trying to do.

Immediate freedom is the freedom (leeway, space, or lack of interference) to do what one is choosing at the present moment. The person attempting suicide is probably confused about what he is choosing at the present moment. A psychologist might get him to see that what he really wants and is choosing is not to die but to achieve something entirely different, e.g., to punish a parent or loved one with whom he is angry. Your taking him by surprise and using force if necessary to save his life may not be an interference with immediate freedom. It might not interfere with his freedom to do what he is choosing to do; for he himself may not be clear on what he is choosing. Rather, it might give him another chance to get clearer understanding about what he really wants.

On the other hand, it can be argued that there are instances of suicide in which the agent *is* making a clearheaded decision. If you are confident that your friend does know what he is doing, then logic will require you to decide to leave him alone.

This example suggests many cases of the same type: Suppose a parent catches a teenager poised to inject himself with heroin. Would it be an interference with the youngster's immediate freedom if the parent grabbed him and stopped him? Perhaps not—despite what was said in the last chapter about drug taking. For it may be that the teenager does not really know what he is choosing to accomplish in the first place.

Or consider a 20 year old girl who has joined a fanatical religious cult. Would her parents be thwarting her immediate freedom if they had a "de-programmer" kidnap her so that he and the parents could lock her in a motel room long enough to talk her into seeing that she was brainwashed by the cult?

How about parents, teachers, or legislators who must decide or rule on homosexuality? Can one logically decide to use force to prevent homosexual activity on the grounds that such acts are always done out of neurotic compulsion and never accomplish what the homosexual really wants to accomplish? This example and perhaps the one about the religious cult show that grey areas exist where there can be much debate over (1) when an agent is clearheaded and knows what he wants and therefore does not need others' help in making his choices, and (2) when he is too immature, neurotic, compulsive, or somehow confused as to what he really wants, and therefore does need others to help him make up his mind.

In other words, an adequate analysis of the application of our theory would lead to much debate over the ambiguous and complicated cases in which it would be difficult to ascertain when one is or is not interfering with someone else's immediate freedom.

Are these complications symptomatic of fatal weaknesses in our theory about not interfering with immediate freedom? No, for we cannot expect moral decision-making to be simple and easy. If the agent is too self-centered to imagine being in another's shoes, or has an axe to grind, e.g., is "out to get" homosexuals, no amount of theoretical understanding can guarantee that he will decide logically. One is always free to rationalize and fool himself into thinking that he is not interfering with someone's immediate freedom when he really is. The job of an ethical theory is not to transform one's character, but to map out how we will make moral decisions insofar as we are willing to be sympathetic and rational.

Accordingly, unless further analysis of hard cases turns up contradictions within our theory or blatant conflicts with common sense or our moral intuitions, then on the strength of our earlier discussion, we will have to conclude that our augmented version of Hare's theory is satisfactory.

RECAPITULATION

Although the study presented in the foregoing chapters provides a historical framework that should be useful for some readers, it is by no means intended to be a complete history of twentieth-century ethics. We have not tried to present a balanced survey of the leading moral philosophers of this century, nor to focus on *which* acts are obligatory or on other ethical issues such as justice, rights, or virtue.

We have concentrated on one key problem which has been largely ignored through the centuries: proving moral obligation, i.e., accounting for ultimate justification. To do this, we analyzed the few philosophers who seemed to come closest in recent years to providing such justification—in hopes of (a) clarifying the concept of ultimate justification and (b) finding such justification or proof.

First, we took a quick look at traditional naturalistic and metaphysical ethical theories, especially utilitarianism and Aristotelian ethics. Next we considered Moore's naturalistic fallacy argument, which revealed the following: that for a theory to account for ultimate justification, it must not assume that some condition or quality such as pleasure or human fulfillment is the same thing as goodness. For then one can still ask whether indeed it is the same.

Nor can we be satisfied with teleological intuitionism à la Moore, which claims to have finally discovered the one thing which can be identified with goodness, namely goodness itself. For, as Prichard demonstrated, even if a theory such as Moore's did put its finger on the ultimate good, the agent could still ask, "*Ought I* to promote that good?" or "Why ought I to do acts which will bring about goodness?" Thus an account of ultimate justification must provide a link to the act itself, or somehow demonstrate that the act itself is right or the agent's duty.

To satisfy or get around the need to provide a "link" between good results and obligation, Prichard said that we can simply intuit that some acts are obligatory—that our minds can "see" that moral obligation pertains to or is a quality of certain acts themselves, such as keeping promises.

Then Ayer showed that such intuitions could be doubted after all. They are unverifiable; and the private nature of such intuitions and the way they conflict among different individuals and cultures also casts doubt on their authenticity. Therefore, an account of ultimate justification must do better than Prichard's theory. It must somehow guarantee the authenticity or certainty of whatever insight or principle it depends on.

After briefly observing how Wittgenstein, Nowell-Smith, and other linguistic analysts picked up the pieces left by Ayer and made a fresh start by focusing on the uses of language, we examined Toulmin's extensive analysis of the uses of moral language. According to Toulmin, if we justify an act by explaining how it harmonizes desires in the community, our justification can be called ultimate. To ask for further justification would be to go beyond moral discourse; for, the very function of moral discourse is simply to give reasons for particular acts in terms of harmonizing desires within the community.

After a chapter of give and take between Toulmin and Hare, we concluded with Hare that Toulmin's attempt to infer moral prescriptions from facts about harmonizing desires actually depended on an implicit prescriptive premise. Toulmin's "rule of ethical inference" itself—

namely that reasons in terms of harmonizing desires are good reasons—served as a prescriptive premise. Since this premise is prescriptive, we now see that we can question it. That is, the fact that reasons in terms of harmonizing desires are always used does not logically entail that we must *prescribe* their use and call them *good* reasons. Their always being used is one thing; our prescribing them and calling them good is something else. Thus, Toulmin's account of justification leaves room for further doubt and questioning: One can still intelligently ask, "Are reasons in terms of harmonizing desires good reasons?" or "*Why* are reasons in terms of harmonizing desires good reasons?" Hare's critique of Toulmin, then, makes it still more clear that for a justification to be ultimate, it must not leave room for additional questions about *whether* or *why* one ought to do the act, i.e., questions which challenge the justification and which the justification does not thoroughly answer.

From this summary, it should be apparent that the survey of selected philosophers from Aristotle to Hare has helped to develop our understanding of what an ultimate justification would have to be like. It would at least have to meet these criteria: (1) It must not be based on the identification of goodness, rightness, or obligation with some other quality or thing such as pleasure. (2) Rather than merely establishing some value or goal as good, the justification must make clear that the act itself is morally obligatory. (3) There must be no possibility of doubt arising about the truth or validity of any intuitions, principles, or other ideas in the justification. It must guarantee its own certainty. (4) Finally, the justification must be self-sufficient in that it leaves no room for

Practical Application and Summary 169

additional questions as to whether or why the person ought to do the act.

Although these four criteria do not necessarily constitute an exhaustive list, they do help us to grasp what an ultimate justification must be like. And, as noted near the end of Chapter 4, we can take the four criteria in order and use them to formulate a concise description of an ultimate justification as follows: It must be a clear and rational demonstration that one ought to do an act; and the demonstration must preclude any doubt about its own truth or validity, as well as any further questioning as to whether or why the agent ought to do the act.

Or, very briefly, an ultimate justification must be a rational demonstration of one's obligation to act which is completely certain and self-sufficient.

* * *

Has Hare's theory filled the bill? He satisfies all of the criteria just listed in that (1) he did not identify any moral quality such as goodness or right with something else such as pleasure. (2) His mode of justification pertains to the very act itself—since he shows how the agent is required by logic to arrive at a moral conclusion such as "I ought not to discriminate against Jones." He shows how the agent must decide to do a particular *act*, not merely to aim at a particular result.

(3) Hare's form of justification does not depend on any intuitions, principles, or other ideas whose truth or validity can be doubted. Instead, it is a function of the very logic of moral reasoning. For example, the agent who is unwilling to be discriminated against under conditions x, y, and z and who thinks clearly and logically is

simply required by logic to decide against discriminating against others under those conditions.

(4) Finally, Hare's account makes it clear that no further questions can be asked that threaten the justification. As mentioned earlier, if the agent asks, "Why must I think logically? Can't I just go ahead and discriminate against Jones?" the answer is that he can. But then he is not engaging in moral discourse; he is opting out of the endeavor of giving reasons or justification for his behavior and of thinking in terms of good, right, and ought. Insofar as he does seriously ask, "Why must I think logically?" or "Why ought I to treat Jones equally?" he is attempting to be logical in his thinking. Such logical thinking will in turn lead him to conclude that he ought not to discriminate against Jones if he is unwilling to have himself discriminated against.

Thus, it seems hard to deny that Hare's theory does finally serve as an account of ultimate justification—as a proof of moral obligation.

Admittedly, Hare has not shown how you, I, and other observers can infer that another agent, or people in general, ought to act in particular ways. As explained near the end of the last chapter, that would involve establishing an objective grounding for morality—or deriving "ought" from "is." Hare has not done that. What he has done is to show how the individual agent will infer that he ought to avoid treating others in certain ways. Therefore, the ultimate justification which Hare has accounted for is limited in the sense that it is restricted to the agent's own viewpoint. In other words, what one agent's inclinations plus logic will require him to decide to do will vary from what logic and another agent's inclinations plus logic will require *him* to do.

Thus, because of the variability of inclinations among

Practical Application and Summary 171

people, Hare argued that there is no one type of behavior that everyone would be required by logic to avoid—so that a true fanatic could logically decide to commit murder. However, thanks to Gewirth's insight and our analysis of immediate freedom, we have, after all, demonstrated that there indeed *is one* type of act which everyone is logically required to decide not to do: Thanks to our inevitable unwillingness to have others thwart our own immediate freedom, all of us, including fanatics, are required by logic not to decide to thwart the immediate freedom of others.

Accordingly, although it was stated at the outset that our purpose is to account for ultimate justification rather than consider what particular kinds of acts are to be justified, we have nevertheless found one type of act or decision which is ultimately justified for all agents: that of not interfering with others' immediate freedom. In other words, for every agent, including the fanatic, the moral obligation not to thwart others' immediate freedom has been proven.

Index

Acceptance, reasons worthy of: Hare and Toulmin, 55–59; Toulmin, 40–52
Accepted practices, Toulmin on, 52n
Acts: facts indicating types and consequences, 89–90n; Hare on justification of, 97–99; Toulmin on justification of, 49–52; types and consequences distinguished, 89–90n; voluntary, and pro-attitudes, 144–45
Addicts, as escaping immediate freedom, 149–51
Agent: relevant factors up to, 123–24; viewpoint of, in deriving ought from is, 154–55
Allen, Paul III, 157n
Analysts. *See* Linguistic analysts
Analytic arguments (Toulmin), 70n
Anarchy and variations in inclinations, 131–32
Application of theory herein, 159–60; complications in, 162–65; examples, 161–62
Arbitrariness of premises and conclusions, 68–69
Arbitrary vs. factual premises, 75–76
Aristotle (384–322 B.C.), 5: on basing morality on facts, 67; and criteria of ultimate justification, 166; on fulfillment, 7; on happiness, 7; on intellectual virtue, 8; on justification, 8–9; on moral virtue, 8; on the practical syllogism, 64; on well-being, 7
Assenting to principles and singular prescriptions (Hare), 113–15
Attitude, morality based on, 69
Ayer, A. J. (b. 1910), 4, 21–27: and criteria of ultimate justification, 66, 167; emotivism of, 27; on ethical reasoning, 61; on good, 22; on intuition, 24–25; *Language,*

Ayer, A. J. (*cont.*)
Truth and Logic by, 23–25; on meaning, 23–25; on Moore, 22, 24–25; on naturalistic fallacy, 25–26; on open question argument, 22; open question argument used by, 26; on Prichard, 24–25; Toulmin on, 38–39; on ultimate justification, 27; on utilitarianism, 22; on verifiability, 23–25

Baier, Kurt, 30
Broad, C. D., on Toulmin, 52n

Categorical imperative (Kant), 126–27
Censuring the true fanatic (Hare), 134–37
Certainty of moral justification, as logical (Hare), 116
Choice: and the clairvoyant, 94–95; ethical theories fail to explain, 84–85; Hare explains, 127–31; inclinations and logic in, 127–31; of moral principles as not arbitrary, 117
Christian ethics, as metaphysical ethics, 11
Clairvoyant, example of, and decisions of principle, 92–94
Coherence, Toulmin on, 52n
Commands, in deduction, 76–78
Community, the: definition of, 46; duty in, 45–48; ethical language used in, 55–59; harmony in and criteria of ultimate justification, 167; Toulmin on, 45–48
Complications in application, of theory herein, 162–65
Conclusions, as prescriptive, 80–83
Conflict in society, and variations in inclinations, 131–32
Confused thinking exploited by fanatics, 136–37
Consequences (Hare): of acts vs. types of acts, 89–90n; checking to test principles, 105–15; in decisions about principles, 97–99; logical, requiring change in moral premise, 110–13; in moral reasoning, 109–10
Considerations as morally relevant, not determined objectively, 123–24
Consistency, justification as a function of, 105–15
Contradiction (Hare): between imperatives, 76–78; justification as a function of, 117; and universalizing of maxims, 126–27
Convenience, Toulmin on, 52n
Correspondence theory of truth, Toulmin on, 40–44
Creditor, example of (Hare), 109–10: and moral reasoning as linear, 128
Criteria of ultimate justification, 15, 29–30, 65–67, 166–69: Hare satisfies, 117, 137,

169–71; and naturalistic fallacy, 15; Prichard on, 21
Cult, example of, and immediate freedom rule waived, 163–65

Deciding about principles ("Decisions of principle," Hare): and the clairvoyant, 92–94; as dependent on prior principles, 99–102; justification of, 87–88, 96–97, 105–6; as justified by facts, 91–94; as not arbitrary, 83; not fully justified, 99–102; relevant factors in, 119–23
Deciding to act, as presupposing immediate freedom, 151–53
Decision: ethical theories fail to explain, 83–85; the factor of, and facts (Hare), 94–99; freedom of, explained by Hare, 127–31
Decision making: ethical theories fail to explain, 84–85; immediate freedom and confusion over purpose, 163–65; role of inclinations in (Hare), 126–27; as strict deduction (Hare), 105–6
Decisions (Hare): justified by logic, principles, and facts, 96–97; as moral or intellectual, 83–85; not fully justified, 99–102
Decisions of principle. *See* Deciding about principles

Deduction: factual or non-factual premises for (Hare), 75–76; among imperatives (Hare), 75–76; linguistic analysts on, 32–33; Popper on, 107–8; Toulmin on, 38–39, 70n
Deontological theories: Frankena on, 71n; as opposed to teleological, 71n
Deontology: Prichard on, 34n; Ross on, 35n; Toulmin on, 46
Deprogrammer, example of: and immediate freedom rule waived, 163–65; thwarting immediate freedom, 149
Description, Toulmin on, 41–44
Descriptive propositions, linguistic analysts on, 32–33
Descriptivism, Hare on: appeal of, 68; and factor of decision, 83–85; and relevant factors, 124
Descriptivism, Hare regressing to, 94–95
Descriptivist theories, unable to explain free choice, 127–28
Desires (Hare): determining relevant factors, 123–25; lead one to reject logical consequences, 123–25; and rejection of prescriptions, 116
Desires, harmonizing (Toulmin), and criteria of ultimate justification, 167

Differences, relevant (Hare), 119–23
Dilemma of factual vs. arbitrary premises, 69, 83
Discrimination, example of (Hare), 116
Disorder in society, Hare on, and variations in inclinations, 131–32
Drug addicts, as escaping immediate freedom, 149–51
Drugs, example of, and immediate freedom rule waived, 163–65
Duty: defined by Moore, 18–19; as function of community (Toulmin), 45–48; Toulmin on, 44–46

Eccentrics, as willing to suffer for ideal (Hare), 134–37
Effects (Hare): and the clairvoyant, 92–94; and decisions of principle, 92–94
Emotivism: Ayer on, 27; Hare's theory as extension of, 101; Toulmin on, 38–39
Emotive meaning, Stevenson on, 27
Entailment among commands (Hare), 77–78
Error in decision making, ethical theories fail to explain, 85
Escape from freedom, in Sartre and Fromm, 149
Ethical properties: linguistic analysts on, 31–33; Toulmin on, 47–48

Ethical reasons, Toulmin on, 48
Ethical theories: application of theory herein, 159–62; as metaethical, 159; as normative, 159
Ethics (Frankena), 71n
Ethics (Moore), 34n
Ethics and Language (Stevenson), 27
Evaluative sentences, appearing as factual (Hare), 82–83
Evolutionary theories, 9
Examples: of immediate freedom rule waived (suicide, drugs, cult, homosexuality), 163–65; of theory herein applied, 161–62
Existentialism, 30, 85–86
Experiment, in scientific reasoning, 107–8
Explanation, Toulmin on, 41–44
Exploration and inclination in individual choice (Hare), 127–31
Exploratory model, explains choice (Hare), 127–31
Exploratory reasoning (Hare): in ethics, 108–10; in science, 107–8
Exploratory use of logic (Hare), 127–31

Factors, relevant (Hare): and fanatics, 134, 137; and immediate freedom, 146–47; up to the individual, 123–27; in judgment, 119–23

Index

Facts, as the basis for moral obligation, 67–69
Facts (Hare): and consequences and types of acts, 89–90n; as key ingredient, 125; justifying decisions of principle, 91–94; in moral reasoning, 109–10; role of, in deciding on principles, 87–88
Facts, values from: Hare on, 61–64; Toulmin on, 59–61
Factual minor premises (Hare), 80–83; as implicitly moral, 82–83
Factual or arbitrary premises, 75–76
Factual sentences (Hare): as implicitly moral, 82–83; as minor premises, 108–10
Fact-value gap, and immediate freedom, 153–55
Fanatics: censuring of, 143–44; as dying for ideal, 134–37; and ultimate justification, 143–44, 171
Fanatics' escaping censure, as flaw in Hare's theory, 134–37
Features, relevant, in judgment: Hare on, 119–23; Kant on, 120–21
Feelings: having regard for others' (Hare), 132–33; morality based on, 69
Foundations of Ethics (Ross), 35n
Frankena: on deontological and teleological theories, 71n; *Ethics* by, 71n

Free action, and pro-attitudes, 144–45
Free choice: how Hare explains, 127–31; inclinations and logic in, 127–31
Freedom and Reason (Hare), 105–39; as consistent with *The Language of Morals*, 108; individual choice explained in, 127–31
Freedom, escape from, 149–51. See also free choice
Freedom, immediate. See Immediate freedom
Fromm, Erich, on immediate freedom, 149
Fulfillment (eudaimonia), Aristotle on, 7
Fulfillment, and criteria of ultimate justification, 166
Function of ethical discourse, Hare and Toulmin on, 55–65
Future prerogatives, contrasted with immediate freedom, 145, 147–49

Gewirth, Alan (b. 1912), 4, 147, 156: and overriding inclination, 144; on deriving ought from is, 153–55; and ultimate justification, 171; works by, 156n
Good: Ayer on, 22; definition of, 12–13; as indefinable, 13; as intuited, 14; as meaning pleasure, 13; Moore, 12–13; open question argument, 13; as a property, 12–13; as a simple quality, 12–13; and ultimate justification, 13–14

Good and ought, gap between, Moore on, 17–19
Goodness, and duty, 14
Good reasons, Toulmin and Hare on, 55–59
Grounds of a judgment, relevant factors for (Hare), 119–23

Happiness, Mill on, 6. *See also* Fulfillment; Pleasure
Harmonizing desires (Toulmin), 46–52, 60–61; and criteria of ultimate justification, 167; as essential in community, 57–59; Johnson on Toulmin, concerning, 70n
Hard cases in application, of theory herein, 162–65
Hare, R. M. (b. 1919), 4, 30, 33: on basing morality on facts, 68; on descriptivism, 68; explains individual choice, 127–31; *Freedom and Reason* by, 105–39; Inaugural Lecture by, 106–7; on Is—Ought gap, 61–64, 170; list of books by and bibliographies, 139n; meets criteria of ultimate justification, 117, 137, 169–71; on moral difference, 62; *Moral Thinking: Its Levels, Method, and Point* by, 138; on Toulmin, 55–69; on Toulmin's Is—Ought derivation, 61–64. *See also The Language of Morals*; *Freedom and Reason*

Hare's ethical theory: application of, 159–62; compared with theory herein, 159
Hedonism, 9; Mill on, 6
Hijackers, as fanatics, 136
Homosexuality, example of, and immediate freedom rule waived, 163–65
Human fulfillment, and criteria of ultimate justification, 166
Hume: on basing morality on facts, 67; on ought from is, 60, 82

Ideals, and fanatics: and ultimate justification, 144; willing to die for, 134–37
Imagining being in another's place, 123, 126–27, 132–33
Imagining logical consequences, and altering moral principles, 111–13
Immediate freedom: and agent's confusion over his purpose, 163–65; contrasted with future prerogatives, 145, 147–49; defined, 145, 147–49; impossibility of giving up, 151–52; overriding value of, 145; and relevant similarity, 146–47; and universalizability, 146–47, 152–53; and ultimate justification, 171; waiving of requirement on, 162–65
Immediate freedom, desire for: unlike ordinary inclination, 151–53
Immediate freedom rule

waived: if agent's purpose is unclear, 163–65; and ultimate justification, 165
Imperative approach, as emotivism (Toulmin), 38–39
Imperatives in deduction, 76–78
Inaugural Lecture (Hare), 106–7
Inclination, overriding, and ultimate justification, 143–44
Inclinations (Hare), 119–38: acceptable consequences determined by, 123–25; concern about others', 132–33; and exploration in individual choice, 127–31; as helping explain free choice, 127–31; importance of, in Hare and Kant, 125; Kant negative about, 126–27; as key ingredient, 125; and rejection of prescriptions, 116; relevant features determined by, 122–23; requiring rejection of a principle, 125; variations in, and disorder in society, 131–32
Inclinations, variations in, and ultimate justification (Hare), 170–71
Indicative form of moral assertions, 78
Indicative statements: linguistic analysts on, 32–33; Toulmin on, 38–39
Individual, as free to choose relevant factors (Hare), 123–25
Individual choice (Hare): in decision, 84–85; exploratory use of logic in, 127–31; how Hare explains, 127–31; inclinations and logic in, 127–31
Induction: linguistic analysts on, 32; Popper on, 107–8; Toulmin on 38–39
Inescapable prescriptive premise, implying absolute ought, 155–56
Intellectual virtue, Aristotle on, 8
Intention, Prichard on, 34n
Interest theories, 9
Intuition: Ayer on, 24–25; good, 14; Prichard on, 20–21, 34n
Intuitionism: and criteria of ultimate justification, 166–67; as objective approach (Toulmin), 38; Ross on, 35n; Toulmin on, 38, 47; unable to explain free choice, 127–31
Is—Ought gap: 67–69; Hare on, 61–64, 170; Hume on, 60, 82; and immediate freedom, 153–55, Toulmin on, 59–61

Jazz trumpeter, example of (Hare), 132–33
Jews, fanatics on (Hare), 135–36
Judgments (Hare): moral, 82; relevant factors in, 119–23
Justification: of acts (Hare), 97–99; Aristotle on, 8–9; Ayer on, 27; criterion of ultimate justification, 15, 29–

Justification (*cont.*)
30, 65–67, 166–69; of decisions of principle (Hare), 96–97, 105–6; definition of, 3–4; definition of ultimate justification, 15; as a function of consistency (Hare), 105–15; as a function of logic (Hare), 117; meaning of, 102; Mill on, 6–7; Moore on, 14–15; of moral principles (Hare), 105–6; of principles, incomplete (Hare), 99–102; of science, Toulmin on, 48–49; Stevenson on, 29; Toulmin on, 48–52, 59; ultimate (Hare), 117

Kant: categorical imperative of, 126–27; on factors relevant in judgment, 120–21; fails to explain willing, 126–27; and Hare on inclination, 125; and kingdom of ends, 11; and metaphysical ethical theory, 11

Language, Wittgenstein on, 32–33
Language of Morals, The (Hare), 61, 75–102, 105: as consistent with *Freedom and Reason*, 108; linear interpretation of, 128; and moral reasoning as rigidly deductive, 128
Language, Truth and Logic (Ayer), 23–25
Law of contradiction, justification as a function of (Hare), 117
Likes and dislikes, others': having regard for (Hare), 132–33
Linear deduction, moral reasoning as (Hare), 128
Linear interpretation, of *The Language of Morals*, 128
Linear model, failure to explain choice by (Hare), 127–31
Linear reasoning, Hare on, 106–7
Linguistic analysts: on induction, 32; on meaninglessness of ethical judgments, 31–32
Link between good and ought: and criteria of ultimate justification, 166–67; Prichard on Moore, 17–19
Logic: exploratory use of (Hare), 127–31; as key ingredient (Hare), 125; linguistic analysts on, 32–33; requiring prescribing of others' immediate freedom, 147
Logical need to reject principles (Hare): due to inclinations, 125; and singular prescriptions, 116
Logical consequences, requiring change in moral premise (Hare), 110–13
Logical contradiction, and universalizing of maxims (Hare), 126–27
Logical criteria: Hare on, 61–64; Toulmin on, 40–52, 60–64

Index 181

MacIntyre, Alasdair, on Aristotle, 9
Major premises (Hare): moral principles as, 108–10; as prescriptive, 80–83
Manager-clerk example (Hare), 109
Maxims: Kant on, 126–27; universalizable without contradiction (Hare), 126–27
Meaning: Ayer on, 23–25; Stevenson on, 29; Toulmin on, 38–39; Wittgenstein on, 32–33
Metaethics, theory herein as, 159. *See also* Linguistic analysts
Metaphysical ethical theories: Christian, 11; Moore, 10; Platonic, 11; Spinoza, 10; Stoicism, 10; Thomistic, 11
Mill, John Stuart (1806–1873), 47, 64, 100: on basing morality on facts, 67; on justification, 5–7; on pleasure, 5–7; on utilitarianism, 5–7
Minor premises (Hare): as factual, 80–83; factual statements as, 108–10
Moore, G. E. (1873–1958), 4–5, 9, 20, 64: Ayer on, 22; on basing morality on facts, 67; criterion of justification from, 66, 166; *Ethics*, 34n; open question argument of, 13; *Principia Ethica* by, 12, 34n
Moral assertions, Hare on: as indicatives or imperatives, 78; deduction among, 79; logical function of, 75–79; as prescriptive, 79; as universal, 114–15
Moral conclusions: as arbitrary, 69; as justified, 69
Moral decisions, role of inclinations in (Hare), 126–27
Moral decision making, as intellectual process (Hare), 84–85
Moral difference, Hare on, 62
Moral judgments. *See* Judgments
Moral obligation: definition of proof of, 3–4; definition of ultimate justification for, 3–4
Moral Obligation (Prichard), 34n
Moral premises: as arbitrary, 68–69; as factual, 68–69; as verifiable, 68–69. *See also* Premises
Moral principles (Hare): arbitrary vs. objective, 83; justification of, 105–6; logical consequences require change in, 110–13; as premises, 105–6. *See also* Principles
Moral reasoning, Hare on: as exploratory, 108–10; as nonlinear, 106–7; as rigidly deductive, 128; as testing principles by checking consequences, 105–15; structure of, 79–83
Moral sentences, appearing as factual (Hare), 82–83
Moral Thinking: Its Levels,

Moral Thinking (cont.)
  Method, and Point (Hare), 138
Moral virtue, Aristotle on, 8
Moral weakness, Hare on: and descriptivism, 84; theories failing to explain, 84–85
Moral words, and commitment to universal rule (Hare), 114–15

Naturalism: defined, 9–10; evolutionary theories as, 9–10; interest theories as, 9–10; of Moore, 9–10; of R. B. Perry, 9–10; of Spencer, 9–10; Toulmin on, 47; unable to explain free choice, 127–28
Naturalistic fallacy: committed by Moore and Prichard, 25–26; and criterion of ultimate justification, 15, 66; and good, 12–14; Moore, 12–14; Moore commits, 19; Prichard on, 19
Nature of a situation, not determining relevant features (Hare), 124
Nazi, as true fanatic (Hare), 135–36
Normative ethical theories, theory herein as not one, 159
Nowell-Smith, P. H. (b. 1914), 30–33, 167: on ethical reasoning, 61; on ultimate justification, 33

Objective approach, as intuitionism (Toulmin), 38
Objective certainty, of justification for Hare, 117
Obligation. *See* Moral obligation
Observer's viewpoint, in deriving ought from is, 153–55
Observing behavior, Toulmin on, 45–48
"On Grading" (Urmson), 51n
Open question argument: Ayer on, 22; Ayer's use of, 26; of Moore, 13; Prichard uses against Moore, 19
Operationism, Toulmin on, 43
Original judgment, relevant factors in (Hare), 119–23
Ought (Hare): as deduced from inescapable prescriptive premise, 155–56; involving commitment to universal rule, 114–15; meaning of, 114–15; defined by good (Moore and Prichard), 17–19
Ought and good, Link between (Prichard and Moore), 17–19
Ought from is, 67–69: Hare on, 61–64, 170; Hume on, 60, 82; and immediate freedom, 153–55; and relevant factors (Hare), 124; Toulmin on, 59–61
Overriding inclination, and ultimate justification, 143–44

Parents, shaping child's principles, 85–86

Perry, R. B., 9, 47
Phenomenology, 30
Philosophical Investigations (Wittgenstein), 32–33
Place of Reason in Ethics, The (Toulmin), 37
Plato (Hare), 138
Platonic ethics, as metaphysical ethics, 11
Pleasure: and criteria of ultimate justification, 166; as meaning good, 13; Mill on, 6; and open question argument, 13
Popper, Karl, on scientific reasoning, 107–8
Pragmatism, Toulmin on, 43
Prediction, Toulmin on, 41–44
Premises (Hare): factual or arbitrary, 75–76; logical consequences require change in, 110–13; as prescriptive and/or objectively based, 83, 105–6. *See also* Minor premises; Moral premises
Prerogatives, future. *See* Future prerogatives
Prescribing (Hare): definition of, 105; one's own actions, 144–45
Prescriptions (Hare): as conclusions, 80–83; as major premises, 80–83. *See also* Singular prescriptions
Prescriptive premises, appearing as factual (Hare), 82–83
Prichard, H. A. (1871–1947), 4–5, 64, 100: on basing morality on facts, 67; and criteria of ultimate justification, 66, 166–67; criticized by Hare, 71n; critique of Moore, 17–19; on deontology, 34n; on gap between good and ought, 17–19, 33n; on intention, 34n; on intuiting rightness, 20–21; on intuitionism, 34n; on justification, 20–21; on knowledge, 20–21; *Moral Obligation* by, 34n; on obligation, 20–21; on ultimate justification, 21
Principia Ethica (Moore), 12: Prichard on, 17–19
Principles (Hare): choice of, not arbitrary, 83, 87–88, 177; factors relevant for, 119–23; logical consequences require change in, 110–13; as major premises, 108–10; not fully justified, 99–102; testing with consequences, 105–15
Prior principles (Hare), 91–94; decisions of principle dependent on, 99–102
Proof of moral obligation, definition of, 3–4. *See also* Justification; Ultimate justification
Propaganda used by fanatics (Hare), 136–37
Properties, ethical: good, 12–13; linguistic analysts on, 31–33; Toulmin on, 37–38

Qualities, ethical. *See* Properties, ethical

Race, and the fanatic (Hare), 135–36
Reason: vs. inclinations for Kant, 126–27; as powerless to cause willing, 126–27. *See also* Logic
Reasoning, moral. *See* Moral reasoning
Reasons as worthy of acceptance (Toulmin), 41–51, 60–61
Reasons in ethics: acceptable vs. accepted, 70n; Toulmin on, 37–52; as worthy of acceptance (Toulmin), 40–52, 55–59
Reasons in science, Toulmin on, 41–44
Rejecting principles and singular prescriptions (Hare), 113–17
Rejection of prescriptions, due to inclinations (Hare), 123–25
Relevant factors. *See* Factors, relevant (Hare)
Relevant similarity: of circumstances (Hare), 126–27; and immediate freedom, 146–47
Religious sects, as fanatical, 136
Respects, relevant in judgment (Hare), 119–23
Responsible decision making, ethical theories fail to explain, 84–85
Responsibility, Hare on, 85–86
Right: defined by Moore, 18–19; involving commitment to universal rule, 114–15
Role of inclinations, in moral decisions (Hare), 126–27
Ross, W. D.: criticized by Hare, 71n; *Foundations of Ethics* by, 35n; on Kant, 120–21
Rule of ethical inference (Toulmin), and criteria of ultimate justification, 167–68

Sartre, Jean-Paul (1905–1980), 85–86: on immediate freedom, 149
Scientific explanation, Toulmin on, 41–44
Scientific reasoning (Hare): as exploratory, 107–8; as nonlinear, 107–8; Popper on, 107–8
Scientific theory, Toulmin on, 52n
Similarities, relevant, 119–23: of circumstances, 126–27; and immediate freedom, 146–47
Singular prescriptions: accepted according to desire, 123–25; moral reasoning more than, 112–15; and rejection of universal prescriptions, 125; and thesis of universalizability, 114–15
Social harmony: O. A. Johnson on Toulmin's view of, 70n; Toulmin on, 37–52
Social practices, justification of (Toulmin), 49–52

Society, disorder in (Hare), 131–32
Spencer, Herbert, 9
Spinoza: on basing morality on facts, 67; and metaphysical ethical theory, 10
Stevenson, Charles L. (1908–1979), 4: on dynamic function, 27; on emotive meaning, 27; *Ethics and Language* by, 27; on justification, 28–29; on meaning, 29; on verifiability, 29; on "working models," 28
Stoics, and metaphysical ethical theory, 10
Substantial arguments (Toulmin), 70n
Suicide, example of, and immediate freedom rule waived, 163–65

Tardy clerk, Hare's example of, 96
Tastes: having regard for others' (Hare), 132–33; variations in, not causing anarchy, 132–33
Teleological intuitionism, and criteria of ultimate justification, 166
Teleological theories: Frankena on, 71n; as opposed to deontological, 71n; Toulmin on, 46
Terrorists as fanatics (Hare), 136
Testing principles, by imagining being in another's place (Hare), 122–23
Theories, ethical. *See* Ethical theories
Theory, scientific, Toulmin on, 52n
Thesis of universalizability (Hare), 114–15; and immediate freedom, 146–47, 152–53
Thinking in terms of principles, as thinking universally, 113–15
Thinking universally: and principles 113–15; requires facing logical consequences, 113–15
Thomists, 67
Thomistic ethics, as metaphysical ethics, 11
Toulmin, Stephen E. (b. 1922), 4, 30, 33, 75, 101: on accepted practices, 52n; on analytic argument, 70n; on Ayer, 38–39; on coherence and convenience, 52n; on community, 45–48; on correspondence theory of truth, 40–44; and criteria of ultimate justification, 167; on deduction and induction, 38–39; on description, 41–44; on deriving ought from is, 59–61; on duty, 44–46; on emotivism, 38–39; on ethical discourse as reason giving, 37–39; on ethical properties, 37–38; on explanation, 41–44; on facts implying values, 59–61; on

Toulmin, Stephen E. (*cont.*)
harmonizing desires, 46–52; on imperative approach as emotivism, 38–39; intuitionism called "objective approach," 38; on justification, 48–52, 59; on justification of science, 48–49; on logical criteria, 40–52; on meaning, 38–39; on observing behavior, 45–48; on physics, 41–44; *The Place of Reason in Ethics* by, 37; on prediction, 41–44, 52n; on reasons in ethics, 44–51; on reasons in science, 41–44; rule of ethical inference, 167–68; on scientific theory, 52n; on social harmony, 37–52; on substantial arguments, 70n; on ultimate justification, 48–52, 65; *The Uses of Argument* by 52n, 70n; and Wittgenstein, 37

True fanatic, as willing to die for ideal (Hare), 134–37

Trumpeter, example of (Hare), 132–33

Ultimate justification: Ayer on, 27; criteria for, 15, 21, 29–30, 65–67, 166–69; definition of, 3–4, 15, 29–30, 65–67; established despite hard cases, 165; Hare accounts for, 117, 137, 169–71; Hare on, 143–44; and immediate freedom, 171; meaning of, 102; Moore on, 19; Nowell-Smith on, 33; Prichard on, 20–21; Toulmin on 48–52, 65; and true fanatics, 143–44; as unattainable, 69. *See also* Justification

Universalizability, and immediate freedom, 146–47, 152–53

Universal principles (Hare): facing logical consequences of, 113–15; meaning of, 114

Universal rule (Hare), commitment to, and use of ought, 114–15

Unpleasant logical consequences, need to face (Hare), 113–15

Unwillingness to give up immediate freedom, as not an inclination, 151–53

Urmson, J. O., 30: "On Grading" by, 51n

Use of ethical language, Hare and Toulmin on, 48, 55–59

Uses of Argument, The (Toulmin), 52n, 70n

Utilitarianism: Ayer on, 22; and criteria of ultimate justification, 166; Mill on, 5–7; as normative, 159

Values from facts: Hare on, 61–64; Toulmin on, 59–61

Variations in inclinations (Hare): not leading to anar-

chy, 131–32; and ultimate justification, 170–71
Verifiability: Ayer on, 23–25; of moral premises, 68–69; Stevenson on, 29
Viewpoint of agent, in deriving ought from is, 154–55
Viewpoint of observer, in deriving ought from is, 153–55
Virtue, intellectual, Aristotle on, 8
Virtue, moral, Aristotle on, 8

Voluntary action, and pro-attitudes, 144–45

Well-being, Aristotle on, 7
Will, and reason and inclination (Kant), 126–27
Wittgenstein, Ludwig (1889–1951), 37, 167: on meaning as use, 32–33; *Philosophical Investigations* by, 32–33
Working models, Stevenson on, 28

Michael J. Zimmerman

AN ESSAY ON HUMAN ACTION

American University Studies: Series V (Philosophy). Vol. 5
ISBN 0-8204-0122-6   335 pp.   pb./lam., US $ 31.00

Recommended prices – alterations reserved

An *Essay on Human Action* seeks to provide a comprehensive, detailed, enlightening, and (in its detail) original account of human action. This account presupposes a theory of events as abstract, proposition-like entities, a theory which is given in the first chapter of the book. The core-issues of action-theory are then treated: what acting in general is (a version of the traditional volitional theory is proposed and defended); how actions are to be individuated; how long actions last; what acting intentionally is; what doing one thing by doing another is; what basic action is; and what omitting to do something is. Attention is also given to the concepts of causation, intention, volition, deciding, choosing, and trying. Finally, a libertarian account of free action is tentatively proposed and defended.

Contents: Three theories: of events; of human action; of free action.

PETER LANG PUBLISHING, INC.
62 West 45th Street
USA – New York, NY 10036